Isle of Man

ELLAN VANNIN VEG VEEN

INCLUDING

DOUGLAS
LAXEY
ST. JOHN'S
KIRK BRADDAN
SNAEFELL
RAMSEY
PEEL
KIRK MICHAEL
PORT ERIN
ST. PATRICK'S ISLE
FOXDALE
PORT ST. MARY
SPANISH HEAD
CASTLETOWN

Geographia Ltd
63 Fleet Street
London, EC4Y 1PE

Guide to Isle of Man
ISBN 0 09 205500 1
© Geographia Ltd.,
63 Fleet Street,
London, EC4Y 1PE

Original manuscript H. O. Wade

Photographic illustrations
by courtesy of
The British Tourist Authority.
Special T.T. Race photographs by
Brian Holden and John Stoddart

Line illustrations by J. Mactear

Series Editor: J. T. Wright

Made and printed in Great Britain by
The Anchor Press Ltd.,
Tiptree, Essex

Dear Reader,

In writing a Foreword to this excellent Guide to the Isle of Man, I am pleased to take the opportunity to welcome the Reader to the Island.

I hope, indeed I am sure, that every visitor to the Isle of Man, whether a newcomer or one who has visited us before, will have an enjoyable and entertaining holiday on our little Island.

The Isle of Man is quite unique; nowhere else can be found, in so small an area, the contrasting scenery to be found here—the verdant landscapes, the open moorland and the rugged coastal views, and all can be taken in by the holidaymaker, whether motoring, cycling or on foot.

Here we have something for everyone, a holiday abroad without the problems of passports, language or currency. I know that you will never regret coming to the Isle of Man for the holiday of a lifetime.

K. M. Halsall.

Mary Halsall, J.P.,
Mayor of Douglas

Contents

Section 1   Introduction

PROVIDING FOR THE NEEDS of the holiday visitor is the most
flourishing industry in the Isle of Man. It is a tribute to the manner in
which this 'industry' is pursued that something like ten times the
number of the resident population flock to this lovely and unique
place each year.

The Isle of Man offers a countryside free from factory chimneys,
heavy lorries and the impedimenta of industrial areas. Consequently
the air is clean and clear and the atmosphere peaceful.

Geographically speaking, Man is an island located in the Irish Sea,
approximately equidistant from the English, Scottish and Irish coasts.
To the south lies the north coast of Wales. The Kingdom extends its
length from Point of Ayre in the north-east, thirty-two miles in a
south-westerly direction to Caigher Point in the Calf of Man. The
greatest breadth north-west to south-east is about eleven miles.

Apart from the flat area in the north the terrain of the Island consists
of hills and mountains with, a little north of the half-way line from
east to west, Snaefell, at 2,034 ft., topping them all. Southwards the
hills are less high but extend right to Spanish Head, enclosing
within their valleys some of the most delightful glens one could
imagine. The heights are grass, heather, gorse and broom covered,
while the valleys are well wooded with a great variety of trees.

There are many rivers and burns, though none of any great size,
but there is some good fishing to be had. However, fishing is not the
most prominent of sports. Where the rivers and streams enter the sea,
there the visitor will discover the greatest beauty and the most
attractive scenes. Indeed, for so small a total area, the Isle of Man
offers attractions and delights out of all relation to its size as well as a
bracing climate which has the effect of giving the visitor an excellent
appetite for his meals and ensures sound sleep at night.

The Manx people appear not to worry unduly about the passage of
time and this makes the tempo of life very restful. Friendliness is
deep-rooted and almost bubbles over, whilst a smiling face is the
order of the day.

The Island is modernised in all essential matters but it retains still
a good deal of the atmosphere, as well as some of the services of the
last century, and this is one of the points which make Man a very
happy place in which to spend a holiday.

The countryside is truly glorious. There is a coastline which for
scenic beauty is difficult to surpass, lovely little towns and villages
await discovery and the city of Douglas is the 'Gateway to the Isle

of Man'. All these aspects make of this small island a superb setting
and an ideal place for those seeking a holiday which is quiet without
being boring, and at the same time ensures modern amenities without
forgetting the old-fashioned pleasures. The Isle of Man Steam
Railway, the Horse Tramway, the Manx Electric Railway—with the
ride to the summit of Snaefell—these together with the exciting
T.T. Motor Cycle Races and many other similar events add lustre to
what is already a very beautiful and delightful Island.

HOW TO GET THERE

By Air: The Isle of Man has a very modern and efficient airport at
Ronaldsway, nine miles south of Douglas. All incoming planes are
met by special transport which conveys passengers to Douglas,
likewise transport from Douglas takes passengers to the airport for
outgoing flights. Public transport operates to other places.

There are year-round services from LIVERPOOL, MANCHESTER,
LONDON, BELFAST, BLACKPOOL, GLASGOW and DUBLIN.
Summer-only flights operate from NEWCASTLE UPON TYNE,
LEEDS/BRADFORD, BIRMINGHAM, EDINBURGH, PRESTWICK,
CARLISLE, CARDIFF, BRISTOL, TEESSIDE, EAST MIDLANDS
AIRPORT, BOURNEMOUTH, STAVERTON, ABERDEEN and
GATWICK.

By Sea: The Isle of Man Steam Packet Company Limited operates
twice-daily sailings during the summer months. They sail between
LIVERPOOL and DOUGLAS. The *Ben-my-Chree, Mona's Queen,
Lady of Man* and the *Manx Maid* are all car carriers with drive-on/
drive-off facilities. Passenger-only ships carry a few cars, but
reservations for vehicles must be made in advance. During the summer
months there are services from ARDROSSAN, FLEETWOOD,
BELFAST, DUBLIN and LLANDUDNO also. In winter only one sailing
between LIVERPOOL and DOUGLAS is maintained.

The Manx Line operates a drive-on/drive-off service from
Heysham, with the *Manx Viking*, daily throughout the year.

ACCOMMODATION

All premises in the Isle of Man where accommodation is offered to
tourists are required to be registered with the Tourist Board for the
Island. There is also a scheme of Voluntary Registration which
requires hoteliers and guest-house proprietors to allow premises to be
inspected for approval by the Isle of Man Tourist Board. Six registers
of such Approved Accommodation are maintained. They are for
Residential Hotels, Private Hotels, Inns, Guest Houses, Furnished
Accommodation for letting to tourists. Holiday Camps and Holiday
Hostels.

All such registered premises are inspected every season by
Inspectors appointed by the Tourist Board.

This constant official scrutiny of holiday accommodation ensures
that the high standard of service and appointment is maintained.

CLIMATE

In the Isle of Man there is, for the most part, a happy absence of
extremes in the weather generally. In the spring, summer and autumn
seasons it would be difficult to match elsewhere the equable
temperatures which are common to the Island. When the sun is hot
there is an almost Mediterranean quality in the sheltered coves and on
the beaches protected by walls of steep cliffs. On the other hand,
for those who do not wish to 'toast' too thoroughly, the cliff roads,
the rolling moorlands and the open country are subject to the fresh,
salty breeziness of the sea, for nowhere in this fortunate island is
one very far from the sea.

Over thirty years the average annual sunshine total at Douglas has
been 1,584 hours, and between April and September recently,
Douglas recorded 1,083 hours of sunshine. The *average* maximum
temperature throughout the Isle of Man is 54 degrees Fahrenheit or 12
degrees Centigrade, and the average minimum is 44 degrees
Fahrenheit or just above 5 Centigrade.

POPULATION

The population consists of some 61,000 souls who occupy an area
of 227 square miles, but it must be noted that two-fifths of the
inhabitants live in Douglas, the capital city and principal holiday area,
and perhaps 10,000 in the larger towns, Ramsey, Peel and
Castletown. This being so, it can be readily appreciated that this
Island provides the holidaymaker with ample room to breathe as well
as plenty of scope for those requiring more lively, sociable
entertainment.

ADMINISTRATION

Man is not part of the United Kingdom, but is an independent
nation, although British people do not need a passport to go there.
It is true that the British Sovereign, as Lord of Man, appoints the
Lieutenant-Governor and through the Privy Council exercises certain
final controls ; however, in all ordinary day-to-day affairs the Island
rules its own destiny through its House of Keys and its Legislative
Council. These bodies, broadly speaking, are the equivalent of the
British House of Commons and House of Lords, but, unlike the U.K.
Parliament, the two Manx Chambers function also as a combined
body called the Tynwald Court.

THE GEOLOGY OF THE ISLE OF MAN

By P. G. Robson, B.Sc.

Despite its insular geographical location, the geology of the Isle of Man is closely related to that of Ireland, Wales, Northern England and Scotland. Three quarters of the Island is composed of metamorphosed sediments of Ordovician age, about 400 million years old. These rocks in particular are closely related to their contemporaries on the mainland, and especially so to those in the Lake District.

At this period in geological history, the distribution of land and sea over the whole of the United Kingdom was completely different from the situation as we see it today. A great sea existed which trended from southern Ireland north-eastwards across the present Irish Sea, and on across the whole of what today is southern Scotland and northern England. Because the rocks that afford us this evidence are so old and contorted, it is difficult to obtain precise information from them to locate the exact positions of land and water at that time. Nevertheless a northern shore, trending SW.–NE. through Girvan, is known to have existed, as well as a parallel southern shore running through Anglesey.

This then being the situation in Ordovician times, it will be apparent that the position occupied by the Isle of Man was in the centre of this ancient sea. The accumulation of ocean floor deposits, known as pelagic sedimentation, was widespread, affecting what is now the Southern Uplands of Scotland, the Lake District, north-eastern Ireland and the Isle of Man. Once the sediments on the Isle of Man had become consolidated into solid rock, they became subjected to various igneous intrusions. Molten magma was forced into these sediments from great depth, and under very high pressure. This magma may have penetrated to the then existing land surface in a few places—if it did so then a volcanic eruption would have taken place. We know from other areas that the whole of this great sea region was subjected to this sort of igneous activity during the Ordovician period.

The evidence for this igneous activity in the Isle of Man can be well seen in the large granite masses at Dhoon and at Foxdale. Two smaller plutonic intrusions also occur on the Island, at Oatland and Ballabunt. The latter differ also in their composition, being less acid (or quartz rich), and therefore cannot be called granites. All four of these major intrusions exist today as solidified rocks of considerable volume. Their surface outcrop may often be large, but cannot allow a true appreciation of the very considerable volume of material involved, simply because we do not know to what depth these bodies extend.

By contrast a second group of igneous intrusions can be found all over the Island—these are dykes. They usually appear as vertical, thin sheet-like bodies of crystalline rock, which again have derived from a molten liquid rock attempting to force its way up to the surface. They tend to move upwards via cracks in the rock, or weak joint planes, or even along the line of old faults. Dykes can be as thin as a few inches, or as wide as several feet. Frequently they can be traced for considerable distances across the countryside. Their differing resistance to weathering, compared to the rocks into which they have been intruded, makes them a particularly conspicuous feature along the shoreline.

The geological birth of the Isle of Man took place during what is known as the Caledonian Mountain Building period. This period of time saw violent earth movements which affected the whole of the northern half of the British Isles. These movements were frequently accompanied by various types of igneous activity. As well as being subjected to these igneous events, the Isle of Man did not escape the effect of the major earth movements either. These earth movements took place over a long period of time, beginning before the first igneous intrusions, and continuing on afterwards. The cumulative result of all this activity is seen today in these rocks, the Manx Slates, which comprise the major proportion of the solid geology of the Island. Strictly speaking they are not true slates, if only because they do not cleave sufficiently well to make roofing slates. In the geological sense of the word, they are a very tough, low grade metamorphic rock.

The folding of the Manx Slates is quite complicated, but essentially they have been formed into large synclines and anticlines, the axes of which run parallel with the length of the Island. The situation becomes particularly interesting when the similar rocks of the Lake District are considered. These are the Skiddaw Slates ('true' slates this time), and are believed to be a north-easterly extension of the same pelagic sediments that originally formed the Manx Slates. Furthermore, the Caledonian Mountain Building activity affected the Lake District as well as the Isle of Man. Anticlinal and synclinal folding can be found in the former which can be correlated across the Irish Sea to the Isle of Man. But one can relate the structure of the Island to even more of the mainland. The reader will recall that the postulated trend of the northern shore for this ancient sea was approximately NE.–SW. This direction is the same as that which the fold axes on the Island follow. It also corresponds to the trend of the Southern Uplands Fault in Scotland, to the Highland Boundary Fault, to the trend of the Great Glen, and to a host of other less conspicuous faults. All these features reflect strain and stress having been accommodated in the earth's crust. Such correlations are typical of areas which have been affected by large mountain-building

episodes. This particular NE.–SW. trend in the British Isles is typical
of the Caledonian orogenic activity. Often a major direction, such
as this one, will be accompanied by a weaker, secondary trend, at
an angle of about ninety degrees.

If we consider the actual topography of the Island, the reader
should now be able to appreciate many of the significant factors in
the shape and trend of the countryside. The Isle of Man is dominated
by a ridge of Manx Slates, which form successively several mountains,
North Barrule (1,860 ft.), Snaefell (2,034 ft.), Beinn-y-phott (1,790 ft.),
Colden (1,599 ft.), and Greeba (1,383 ft.) in the north, and to the
south Slieau Whallian (1,094 ft.), South Barrule (1,585 ft.), and
Cronk ny Arrey Laa (1,449 ft.). This large and almost continuous
ridge is broken only once, by a valley which connects Peel on the
west coast with Douglas on the east. This is a valley formed as the
result of two streams working backwards towards one another. They
were both obviously exploiting the same line of weakness in the rock.
The trend of this valley is interesting to note, being almost at right
angles to the trend of the mountain ridge.

Physiographically, the Isle of Man can be divided into two areas.
Comprising the bulk of the Island are the Manx Slate mountains,

Kitterland Sound and the Calf of Man

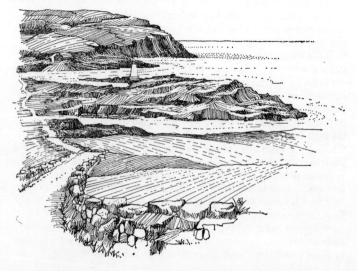

but in the extreme north there is a roughly triangular area of unconsolidated glacial drift deposits forming a quite separate and distinct part of the Island. Nowhere does the topography exceed 350 ft. The transition between this area and the mountain chain is a very rapid change in slope. The low lying plain abuts sharply against the Manx Slates, which rise rapidly to a height of about 1,000 ft. This conspicuous topographic feature is the result of an old shore line which used to run due west of Ramsey, around the foot of the mountains, via Sulby and Ballaugh and thence to the present western coast of the Island.

This old shore line, together with the approximate shape of the rest of the Island as it can be seen today, is believed to have marked the extent of the Isle of Man immediately prior to the onset of the Ice Age. The Irish Sea as a whole was covered by a very large and thick ice sheet, which moved slowly in a southerly direction. The considerable erosional effect of the ice can be seen by scratches and grooves which mark nearly every outcrop of solid rock on the Island. It is perhaps worth mentioning that this scratching is not made by the ice itself moving over an outcrop of rock, but by rocks and boulders that are frozen solid into the body of the ice. The marks of this glacial erosion can even be seen on the summit of Snaefell itself, which means that this Irish Sea ice sheet must have been at least 2,000 ft. thick, and was probably even thicker than this in places.

Despite the great size of the ice sheet that moved over the Island, the drainage pattern was little altered. This had already become well established before the onset of the Ice Age. Nevertheless the effect of such a large ice sheet moving over the countryside can still be clearly seen today. Most obvious is the drift plain to the north of the Island. The glacial debris of which this area is composed was scooped off the floor of the Irish Sea to the north of the Island, and then piled up against its northern end. These sea-floor deposits are inextricably mixed up with the rest of the land-derived boulder clay. The Bride Hills, around the village of Bride, are typical of gently rounded boulder clay hills, shaped by the moving ice. In areas where the boulder clay can be seen, the observer will notice that it is composed of all shapes and sizes of rock fragments, ranging from silt up to large boulders. These boulder clays lack any form of size-sorting whatsoever. These typical glacial deposits can be seen all over the Island—around the coast, and often fringing the sides of mountain valleys. Fragments of the Foxdale and Dhoon granites can sometimes be found south of their respective localities, evidence that the ice action plucked pieces of rock from the outcrops, and carried them varying distances away, but always in a southerly direction.

In the south-west corner of the drift plain, just beside Ballaugh, there is a low-lying marshy area of land known as the Curragh. During post-glacial times this area of land was covered by one or more freshwater lakes, remnants of the melting ice. These lakes slowly drained away through the encircling boulder clay, cutting small channels for themselves, notably along the course of the present Killane River.

With the retreat and final disappearance of the ice sheet, the Sulby River found itself faced with a large glacial drift plain where once it had disgorged itself straight into the Irish Sea. Today the river turns due east once it has left the Sulby Glen, making its way along what was the old pre-glacial shore line, and enters the sea at Ramsey. Apart from this example, the rest of the Island drainage has remained largely unaffected by the ice ages.

Apart from the Manx Slates, there are two small areas in which another group of rocks is found. These are of Lower Carboniferous age, being much younger than the Ordovician rocks. There are exposures of rock near Castletown in which this 'uncomfortable' relationship between the Ordovician and Carboniferous strata can be studied. They provide a marked contrast to the metamorphic slates. The Carboniferous rocks outcrop as flat-lying or gently dipping, non-metamorphic sediments, whereas the underlying Manx States are steeply folded. The largest area of Carboniferous is in the region of Castletown, where immediately one can notice a more subdued character to the landscape. Here the rocks are mostly of limestone, lying above a basalt conglomerate. Fossils can be found, and are most likely to include goniatites, corals and brachiopods. This is another feature which contrasts with the Manx Slates—the latter possess a complete dearth of fossils. A few worm casts and burrows may perhaps be found, and very occasionally a fragment of a trilobite, but little else.

The second locality in which rocks of the Carboniferous occur is on the west coast around the village of Peel. This rock is mostly composed of red sandstone, with occasional beds of conglomerate and impure limestone. What few fossils that do occur are usually some form of coral. This sandstone provides the only freestone for the Island, with which the Castle and Cathedral of Peel have been built.

In conclusion, therefore, it may be said that the Isle of Man is dominated by old, very tough metasediments, which outcrop over the whole of the Island. It is these which are responsible for the strikingly rugged appearance of the coastline, and the equally impressive ridge of mountains which runs along the length of the Island. Superimposed on these Ordovician sediments are two localised outcrops of Carboniferous rocks, giving, by contrast, a markedly subdued topography. The final addition to the shape of the landscape was the deposition of glacial debris, and most notably so in the northern sector.

WILDLIFE OF THE ISLE OF MAN

By W. Balmain

Perhaps the most exciting thing when one visits an island no larger than the Isle of Man is that one can get to know it intimately in quite a short space of time.

This island, so close to the mainland, is particularly interesting from the natural history point of view—not so much because it is filled with unusual species but for two very specific reasons. Firstly, it was completely cleared of quadrupeds during the glacial period, and occupied only by those that crossed the remaining land bridge in post-glacial years before that bridge disappeared beneath the waves. Secondly, one may assume that man was responsible for the introduction of a good proportion of the many species found today.

There are, for example, no toads or newts, no snakes, moles, foxes or squirrels, and it is interesting to note how records have been handed down.

HEDGEHOGS arrived on a schooner wrecked in 1805, and were given to the Islanders as pets. They have since spread throughout the Island.

THE BLACK RAT came on a Russian ship wrecked during the nineteenth century.

RABBITS were introduced by the retainers of the Derby family.

THE TAIL-LESS MANX CAT was brought to the Island by a sailor.

Birds of course have their own means of transport and consequently we find, within the space of a few miles, a wonderful collection of sea, cliff-dwelling, moorland, meadow and woodland varieties. Hawks feature in the Island's history to the extent that in 1405 King Henry IV gave the kingdom of the Island to Sir John Stanley on homage of two falcons—to be repeated by his heirs on the day of their Coronation. This practice continued until the year 1821.

Migrants of course are constantly seen on the island, two important watchpoints being from Langness and the Calf of Man; the latter has an observatory and is a National Trust area whilst the former is sanctuary to varieties of water-fowl. Warblers, swallows, swifts, martins, finches, linnets, siskin, yellow and corn buntings, meadow and rock pipits, robins and wheatears can be seen in season. Winter brings the thrush family of redwing and fieldfare whilst swelling the population of resident blackbirds, song and mistle thrush. An occasional ring ouzel may be observed in the higher land together with the twite and, even less occasionally, the short-eared owl is observed adding to the resident owl family of barn and long-eared owls.

By the rivers, pied, yellow and grey wagtails are seen and the heron, a resident, breeding in small numbers, compared with that other expert fisherman, the kingfisher. The wren has two other small birds for company—the goldcrest and tree creeper—but this company is not encouraged because there are few great stands of timber. Paradoxically, wood pigeons are a common sight.

Crows are well represented, the largest of the family, the raven, breeds on the cliffs and high sites inland; even the now rare chough breeds on the cliffs. Magpies, rooks, hoodie crows and jackdaws are found throughout the Island but only a few carrion crows are residents. Kestrel, merlin and sparrow hawk are outshone by the dashing peregrine falcon—the first bird incidentally to appear in the Manx records.

Blue, long-tailed, great and cole tits add their splash of colour everywhere but the shoreline, with its host of sea birds, has special charm—winter swelling the numbers of waders—curlew, whimbrel, sandpiper, little stint and sanderlings are a few. Golden plover, lapwing and ringed plover are seen in numbers. Common and jack snipe can be observed easily; woodcock too, become more numerous in winter time. Oyster catchers send their calls echoing along the shore.

Grey-lag and barnacle are perhaps the most common geese, and ducks—mallard, teal, widgeon, shoveler, tufted, pochard and goldeneye —vary their numbers with the passing seasons. Great northern divers are regularly observed in winter. Fulmar petrels, terns, gannets, cormorant, shag, razorbills, guillemots puffins and gulls of many kinds provide an endless source of joy to the ornithologist.

Red grouse and partridge may be found inland but the pheasant appears to be surprisingly rare. Mute swans are resident and whooper swans as well as Bewick's appear riding the cold winter winds.

Before leaving the birds, a visit to the curragh lands should be made, those less populated and undisturbed places, to hear the dawn chorus of the nesting birds.

As for mammals the Island is poorly represented; the stoat, brown and black rat, pigmy shrew, long-tailed field and house mouse are here. Hares similar to the Irish hare run the fields, and hedgehogs are quite numerous. Pipistrells are the most numerous of the bat family which is also represented by the long-eared and natterer's bats. Porpoise known by the not very complimentary Manx name of 'muc-varrey' present a splendid sight as they leap in the bays and the grey seal is often seen on the rocky shores and beaches. The rabbit survives despite its devastation by myxomatosis.

Heather covers the hills, cotton grass warns of marshy and boggy ground, bluebells light up the glens and ferns crowd in to the verge of path and road. Manx cabbage, thrift and sea campion skirt the coastline and we must not forget the Manx national flower—the Ragwort.

Manx sheep or Loghtan sheep still exist, but only a very few. You may see them at the Cregneish Folk Museum. The male, with four horns, is a most unusual sight. Manx tailless cats interbreed with the domestic so that we may find domestic as well as feral cats with normal, short or no tail at all! Another tailless creature, a fowl, is still to be seen on old farms.

Red deer are extinct as are the giant Irish elk whose massive remains have been found on the Island.

Salmon run in from the sea on the silver highways of the rivers and trout may be found in the smallest stream.

The visitor should round off his 'wild life tour' of the Island by visiting the Curragh Wild Life Park, Ballaugh, and the natural history gallery of the Manx Museum in Douglas.

Loghtan Sheep

HISTORY

The first known inhabitants of the Isle were the early Stone Age people. These were followed by the later and more advanced users of stone tools and implements, many of which, together with samples of Stone Age pottery, have been found and can be seen now in the Manx Museum in Douglas.

Then the Bronze Age folk arrived, leaving evidence of their presence in the many burial places which have been found throughout the Island.

The people of the Iron Age have left far more impressive earthworks forts and burial cairns of a most distinctive character; these were the Celts, who had, perhaps, the greatest influence upon the life and character of the Manx people.

Christianity, which, tradition says, was introduced by St. Patrick and St. Maughold, arrived around the fifth or sixth centuries. Some two hundred ruins of the earliest Christian churches, or keills, are to be found on the Island. A great many have been excavated and may be visited. In addition there are several collections of early Celtic crosses, many showing very fine workmanship.

The Vikings made their first contact with Man towards the end of the eighth century and thereafter made various raids which were, at first, piratical invasions for loot and plunder. Later the Norse colonists arrived, settled and inter-married, bringing with them, of course, their own customs and particular skills, all of which are now an intrinsic part of Manx life. Thus began a period of Norse rule which lasted until the thirteenth century.

During this period the Kingdom of Man included the Out-Isles, or Hebrides, of which there were said to be thirty-one islands. Had all the islets been counted the number would have been several hundreds.

The Out-Isles sent sixteen members to the House of Keys, as did Man, giving a total of thirty-two members. In the twelfth century, after a battle off Colonsay, the Out-Isles were divided and the Kingdom of Man retained only the groups represented by Lewis and Skye, which, thereafter, sent eight members to the House of Keys, so reducing the number of Members to twenty-four, the number remaining to this day.

In the thirteenth century the Kingdom of Man passed to Scotland, so that the House of Keys contained only sixteen members from Man itself. However, the Keys apparently refused to consider the separation as final and, to keep the seats of the Members from the Out-Isles, appointed eight extra members from Man, thus keeping the original twenty-four seats.

The Tynwald, or combined House of Keys and Legislative Council, one of the most ancient of Parliaments, dates from the early Norse

colonisation and remains virtually unaltered apart from the number of
seats in the House of Keys.

Extensive Smuggling

After the final defeat of the Norsemen at the Battle of Largs (1263),
the Island became a shuttlecock, possession passing to and fro
between England and Scotland. In 1403 the English finally took
control and John Stanley, whose grandson became the first Earl of
Derby, was made Lord of Man. So began some 350 years of rule by
the Stanleys. Nine Earls of Derby held the title until the male line
became extinct. It then passed to the Duke of Atholl with whom it
remained until 1765, when the English government, in order to put
an end to the very extensive smuggling which had developed,
purchased the regal rights.

A few years later the Duke's remaining rights were purchased
and since then the Island has been administered by a combination
of the Island's own government, and a Lieutenant-Governor appointed
by the British Monarch.

THE POST OFFICE

The Island Postal Authority issues its own postage stamps. These are
accepted by members of the Universal Postal Union.

A full set of Definitive Stamps of sixteen denominations, ranging
from ½p to £1 has been introduced and from time to time special
Commemorative issues are available.

Philatelic supplies, and further information, is obtainable from:—

The Isle of Man Post Office Authority,
P.O. Box 10.M.
Douglas, Isle of Man
Telephone: Douglas 23280

ELLAN VANNIN VEG VEEN

The name Isle of Man is, in Manx Gaelic, Ellan Vannin or Ellan
Vannin Veg Veen—'The Dear Little Isle of Man'.

Where the name originated it is impossible to say but it seems
likely that it has some reference to a hilly or mountainous place.
There have been a number of variations of the word 'Man'; at one
time the Norsemen called the Island 'Mon' or 'Maon', while Caesar
referred to 'Mona' and the Welsh to 'Manaw'. Some have suggested
that the name comes from Manannan, a Celtic god of the sea.

Three Legs

The well-known Manx escutcheon, the Three Legs, are called
'Trie Cassyn', and this symbol dates, as the Island Coat of Arms,

probably from the twelfth or thirteenth centuries. Prior to that time it had been used by the Norse kings. The Isle of Man had used a ship on its official seals. The motto surrounding the 'Three Legs' is 'Quocunque Jeceris Stabit', which means 'Whatsoever way you may throw it, it will stand'. (See back cover of this Guide.)

AGRICULTURE

After tourism, the second largest industry, both in size and importance, is agriculture. Because it is an island of grass, the emphasis is on cattle and sheep-rearing; dairying and fattening are about equally important. Generally, Friesians are favoured for milk-production while Herefords crossed with Friesians provide the basis for beef-production. Large numbers of fat cattle are exported, but virtually no stores are included in this export trade. A number of Irish stores are the only cattle imports so that in this respect the Island is very nearly self-supporting. Fortunately, it is, so far, free from disease.

Black-faced sheep are the only inhabitants of the hill-tops, while the lower slopes are given over to the Cheviots or Suffolk–Leicester cross.

A considerable acreage of corn is grown, the largest crop by far being oats, with wheat and barley a very long way behind. While a fair acreage of root-crops is grown for feeding, carrots are grown for sale in the sandy northern part of the Island.

The climate makes conditions difficult for corn-growing but, on the other hand, it is ideal for grass.

FISHING

There was a time when fishing was the chief industry, but in recent years it has fallen to third place in importance. This decline has been caused because of the use of large modern trawlers with mother-ships, by the United Kingdom and Continental countries. Whatever its port of origin the individual herring-drifter or trawler has little chance of survival in this age of ultra-mechanisation and huge capital outlay.

In the season, foreign boats fish the Irish Sea and the North Atlantic, selling their catches in both Douglas and Peel. However, the Isle of Man collects harbour dues and sales commission from this combined import and export trade.

There are, of course, a few Manx boats which still fish for herring. Smaller boats fish also for white fish—both inshore and deep-sea—but the number has declined sadly.

There is a considerable business in the fishing, processing and exporting of scallops and queenies. This is a very popular type of shell-fish, the correct name of which is 'tanrogan'. Queenies are a smaller variety. This trade constitutes a very welcome increase in the Island's exporting business and is, in addition, a means of keeping a number of boats working which would, otherwise, be laid up.

OTHER INDUSTRIES

There are woollen mills and a number of light manufacturing industries which, combined, add considerably to the income of the Island without marring the environment. In fact, Man is quite remarkably free from any such blemish.

INTERNAL TRANSPORT

The Douglas Bay Horse Tramway

The Douglas Bay Tramway was founded by Thomas Lightfoot, and commenced operation on 7 August 1876 with a 'fleet' of three horse-drawn vehicles. At that time the service operated between the Sefton Hotel and Burnt Mill Hill (now called Summer Hill).

In 1877 the service was extended to its present terminus opposite the Peveril Hotel, and in 1882 the tramway became a public company.

In 1894, when the fleet of cars had expanded to twenty-nine horse-drawn vehicles, the concern became the property of the Isle of Man Tramways and Electric Power Company. The over-ambitious plans of this company had, by the year 1900, brought about its financial collapse, but the horse-drawn tramway survived, and operates to this day with its northern terminus now at Derby Castle —the southern terminus of the Manx Electric Railway.

Two types of car are used, one is closed, the other open and known affectionately as 'toast-racks'—a most apt description.

The Manx Electric Railway

Between 1894 and 1900 The Isle of Man Tramways and Electric Power Company (mentioned above) constructed lines from Douglas to Laxey and Ramsey, to the Snaefell Mountain Summit, and built a cable-drawn tramway to Upper Douglas. After the financial collapse of the company the two Douglas lines were taken over by the Corporation of Douglas, and in 1929 the cable tramway was closed.

The Manx Electric Railway Board of Tynwald now operates services which run on double-track standard-gauge lines northward from Douglas to Laxey.

The route of the line to Ramsey runs through some enchanting scenery, at times very near the coast. Several steep gradients are negotiated.

The Snaefell Mountain Railway is an unique achievement and the only electrically powered mountain railway in the British Isles. From Laxey it climbs from a height of 119 ft. above sea-level to an

altitude of 1,990 ft. at the mountain summit, all in a distance of just
over four miles. Gradients vary from one in twelve (over more than
three-quarters of the journey) to only one in forty-two.

The terminus is a short and easy fourteen yards from the actual
summit. On a very clear day not only can the whole of the Island be
seen from this vantage point but also the coasts of Scotland,
England and Wales, from the Mull of Galloway to the Isle of Anglesey
and, to the west, the coast of Ireland.

The Isle of Man Steam Railway Company

There was talk of constructing a railway in the Isle of Man as long
ago as 1864. A survey made at the time indicated that there should
be ample traffic but no further move was made until 1870, when a
dozen Manx businessmen sat down to formulate proposals for
building lines from Douglas to Castletown, Peel and Ramsey.

As a result of their efforts the Isle of Man Railway Company was
registered on 19 December 1870, with a capital of £200,000.

Twelve months later only £30,000 of this sum had been subscribed;
however, the remainder was obtained from sources outside the
Island, the Duke of Sutherland playing a principal part.

In 1872 contracts were signed for the construction of a line to
Peel, and another to Port Erin.

The level track through Braddan, Union Mills, Crosby and St.
John's to Peel was the first to be completed, and it was officially
opened on 1 July 1873. By some quirk of fate the company's first
engine, a Beyer-Peacock 2-4-0 named 'Sutherland' (after the Duke),
seemed reluctant to stay on the rails. This somewhat prolonged the
ceremony, but the next day, when normal passenger traffic commenced,
'Sutherland' gave no further trouble.

The following year the line to Castletown and Port Erin was opened,
giving the railway company a total length of track of twenty-seven
miles with, at this time, five locomotives and fifty wagons and
coaches.

By now the idea of a line from Peel along the west coast and
across the flat northern neck of the Island to Ramsey had been
abandoned. However, the people of Ramsey, not wishing to be left
out of the railway business, formed their own company, which was
registered in 1878 as the Manx Northern Railway Company, built
the line, and commenced a passenger and goods service on
23 September 1879.

A further length of track between St. John's and Foxdale came
into operation and was operated by the Manx Northern Railway from
17 August 1886.

After only a few years, demand for these lines declined and the
Manx Northern Railway was eventually taken over by the Isle of
Man Railway Company, which then had a route mileage of forty-six

and a quarter, a figure which was never exceeded.

The development of the internal combustion engine and the consequent growth of road transport was a severe blow to the railway, and by 1965 much of the permanent way was so badly in need of repair that the railway had to be closed.

Now, with Manx Government financial aid, the line between Douglas and Port Erin is preserved by the Isle of Man Railway Company who run services during the summer. It runs through many of the most popular resorts, is the longest railway of its kind in the British Isles, and has proved a great attraction to all who visit the island. Unfortunately, the future of this remaining line is uncertain and it too may become only a memory.

A very fine little booklet, *Railways in the Isle of Man*, tells the story of these railways, the Isle of Man Steam Railway as well as the two Electric Railways, in considerable and extremely interesting detail.

Of course, modern coach and bus services operate throughout the Isle of Man, and for those who prefer private transport, cars may be transported to the island, or hired upon arrival. Road surfaces are excellent, and garage facilities abundant.

THE ISLE OF MAN STEAM PACKET COMPANY

One of the unique Manx institutions is the Isle of Man Steam Packet Company Limited, for the Company was founded by Manxmen, its fleet has always been captained by Manxmen and the crews have always been Manxmen. An Island community must necessarily value all means of continuing communication with the nearest mainland both for trade and for leisure and pleasure pursuits. Despite the rapid growth of airways concerns the ships are always needed. They have built up a reputation for reliability no matter what the weather and when many an air service is grounded the famous boats of the Isle of Man Steam Packet Company butt their way through the Irish Sea to arrive or depart no more than a little late whatever the storms may have been. Rarely indeed has this celebrated Company suspended even one of its sailings.

As long ago as 1819 the first steamer service began plying between Britain and the Island. This ship was out of Whitehaven in Cumberland and not very fast and was soon being challenged by a steamer out of Greenock called the *Robert Bruce*. This vessel offered a weekly return service but was soon to be challenged in its turn from Liverpool by the James Little boats with a three-times-weekly schedule! The growing popularity of the Isle of Man as a place of resort for the prosperous mill-owners and workers of Lancashire and Yorkshire, as well as the people from the Potteries in the Midlands, continued to stimulate these rivalries. Readers of Arnold Bennett will recall the wry snobberies of the 'Five Towns'

where his colourful characters discussed the possibilities of their
holiday visits to the Isle of Man, for this was a day and age when to
be able to afford a holiday was a sign of having 'arrived' socially.

In the course of these boom years the people of Man, wishing to
set up a much superior service to any existing, formed a private
company in order to provide better schedules. The first such boat
was called *Mona's Isle*, and this was also the original name of the
company. Only 116 ft. long the *Mona's Isle* sailed under Captain Gill.
She had a beam of 19 ft., a depth of 10 ft. and a displacement of
200 tons. In the Manx Museum at Douglas the ship's bell of the first
Mona's Isle is on show.

After a time the Company was re-formed and reconstituted as the
Isle of Man Steam Packet Company, and then began the fine fleet of
ships built by the celebrated Napier Shipyard. As the older boats
were scrapped each new vessel was hailed as better than its pre-
decessor, as they were, indeed, a remarkable series of boats. Some
of the names were as famous in the rest of the United Kingdom as in
the Island itself. The *King Orry, Mona II, Fenella, Snaefell, Viking,
Ben-my-Chree, Manxman* and *Tynwald* became as familiar names in
the docks and harbours of Liverpool, Llandudno, Belfast and Dublin
as they were in Douglas and Ramsey.

One of the most famous ships was the *Ellan Vannin*, of 339 tons.
This vessel had sailed for twenty-three years as the second *Mona's
Isle*, when, as a paddle-steamer she was the mascot of the fleet.
In 1883 she was converted to a screw-steamer, renamed the *Ellan
Vannin,* and resumed regular sailings for many years, during which
period she gained a tremendous reputation for her time-keeping,
even in the roughest weather. Once, when a score of ocean-going
liners were sheltering in Ramsey Bay, the *Ellan Vannin* threaded her
way out, steamed to Whitehaven and returned in the evening to be
welcomed by the sirens of the other ships still sheltering there !

Tragically, the bold little *Ellan Vannin* was at last beaten by the
rough weather she had braved so often. On 3 December 1909 she
steamed out of Ramsey heading for Liverpool, with fourteen passengers
and the usual complement of mail, cargo and crew. At the Mersey
Harbour Bar she was hit by a force 12 gale from the north-west and
foundered with a total loss of life. She must have been utterly
overwhelmed by a gigantic wave for when the wreck was examined
she was found to be upright in 70 ft. of water, with the captain's
bridge swept away and her decks stove in. In all the history of the
Steam Packet Line this was one of the very few peace-time losses the
Company sustained. Naturally, the name *Ellan Vannin* has never been
repeated.

The fastest ship the Line ever owned was the *Ben-my-Chree*, of
2,650 tons, built in 1908. At her trials she reached speeds of 26·9
knots; her mean average time between the Bar Lightship and

Douglas Head was 2 hours, 24½ minutes. Her record-breaking run, made in 1909, from Liverpool landing-stage to Douglas in 2 hours, 57 minutes, has not been rivalled to this day.

All the wonderful ships of the Isle of Man Steam Packet Company went into service with the Royal Navy in two World Wars. The *Ben-my-Chree* made a fast run from England to East Africa to deliver explosives for the sinking of the German cruiser *Königsberg*, which was sheltering in the River Refugi. *Ben-my-Chree's* average speed on this occasion was over 22 knots, including necessary stoppages for recoaling, etc. Later she served as a seaplane carrier in the Mediterranean but was bombarded and sunk off Castellorizo by the guns of a Turkish battery. In 1920 she was raised and refloated, but was sold and taken to Piraeus, the port of Athens, where she was broken up. A forlorn end to such an outstanding history.

Another famous ship from the Manx Steam Packet Company, the *King Orry* will always be remembered for having led the German Fleet into Scapa Flow for the surrender in 1918. In the Second World War all these sturdy vessels again did yeoman service for the British Navy and doubtless many a soldier, stranded on Dunkirk Beach in 1940, felt hope revive at the appearance on the scene of ships normally associated with home and holidays!

Waterfall, Sulby Glen

Section 2   Holiday Pursuits

FACILITIES FOR A GREAT variety of holiday activities are available in the Isle of Man. Apart from the well-known spectator events which take place during every holiday season, opportunities exist for the visitor to participate in recreations of his own choosing. Details of some of these are given below. Other tourist information is available from the offices of the Isle of Man Tourist Board, established at 13 Victoria Street, Douglas. In the summer season, an Information Bureau is open daily at the Sea Terminal in Douglas.

MOTORING
The 'Rule of the Road' in the Isle of Man is drive on the left, overtake on the right and you do need to be in possession of a valid Driving Licence, or International Driving Permit, if you bring a car into the Island. Visitors from the United Kingdom must ensure that the vehicle is currently licensed in the United Kingdom.

A temporary visitor is permitted to have a car on the Island for twelve months without liability to further Road Tax provided that the vehicle is used only for personal travel.

To the motorist from the mainland where crowded roads and traffic jams are commonplace, the Isle of Man will seem a paradise. The Island is well endowed with roads and those between the main centres are good, fairly wide highways, while the remainder are safe, well-surfaced pleasant roads and lanes. With considerably less lorry traffic, and none of the very large vehicles which have become all too familiar in Britain, the narrower Manx roads are as safe as a three-lane highway—and a great deal more enjoyable to drive on.

During the T.T. races in June and the Manx Grand Prix in September the course is closed to other vehicles. Many thousands of spectators line the route to see some of the most thrilling racing in the British Isles. Those interested will find details of the best vantage points in the section of this guide book entitled 'The Tourist Trophy and Manx Grand Prix Races'. The motorist should remember that there are a number of level-crossings over the Manx Electric Railway, most of which are controlled by crossing lights.

Speed limits: There are 40 m.p.h. and 30 m.p.h. speed limits in urban areas in the Isle of Man and in a few villages there is a 20 m.p.h. restriction, but in any case it is wise to drive slowly and with great care in such places as many streets are narrow and thus afford little room for vehicles to pass each other. This means single-line traffic, sometimes, where you least expect it.

Holiday Pursuits

Traffic lights: There are not very many places where traffic lights have been installed in Man. HOWEVER: Take special note of the many STOP signs for these control most of the pedestrian road-crossings. TAKE SPECIAL CARE TO OBEY THESE SIGNS.

Parking: In the Isle of Man it is an offence to park a car or any vehicle within the area marked by a white line painted in the centre of the roadway and it is also forbidden to park anywhere in a street if there is a designated car-park nearby. In fact the car MUST be parked in such a car-park. Where parking is permitted in public streets there is a sign indicating the hours and length of time such parking is allowed. Where there is a single yellow line a car may only stop (between 8 a.m. and 6 p.m.) for setting down or picking up goods or passengers. Where there is a double yellow line, waiting is prohibited except for the setting down or picking up of goods or passengers.

Car Hire: For those who prefer to hire a car on arrival there are ample vehicles available. The following firms each have a fleet of modern vehicles and operate an all-Island service.

Athol Garage (1945) Ltd., Hill Street, **Douglas**
E. B. Christian Ltd., Bridge Garage, **Douglas**
Central Motors Ltd., Circular Road, **Douglas**
'U' Drive Car Hire, Peveril Buildings, **Douglas**
Mylchreests Motors Ltd., Westmoreland Road, **Douglas**
Paul Hardinge Ltd., Peel Road, **Douglas**
E. B. Christian Ltd., Airport Garage, **Castletown**
Mylchreests Motors Ltd., Lezayre Road, **Ramsey**
Raymotors, Parliament Square, **Ramsey**
Empire Garage Ltd., Peveril Road, **Peel**
Shore Garages Ltd., Station Road, **Port Erin**
Shore Garages Ltd., Shore Road, **Port St. Mary**

CAMPING AND CARAVANNING

There are camp sites and Youth Hostels in the Isle of Man, details of which may be obtained from the appropriate organisations in the United Kingdom.

With regard to caravan holidays there is some restriction on the period of stay and on the type of caravan permitted to use the Manx roads. Consult your motoring organisation for current details.

WALKING

For those who prefer to explore on foot, the Isle of Man may be classed as almost ideal. At no point is one more than three miles from a road and although the contours in this hilly island are steep in places the heights are not great. Snaefell is the only mountain over 2,000 ft., and its summit is only one mile from a main road. There are twenty-three heights between 1,000 and 2,000 ft. and numerous lesser ones.

The law of trespass and right-of-way is similar to that in England. There are many miles of excellent footpaths, many more that are less well defined, and acres of open, unenclosed moorland and hills where the sensible walker who follows the 'Country Code' and treats the countryside with respect, is ever welcome to roam as he pleases.

Always carry map and compass.

SEA ANGLING

One of the popular attractions of the Island is fishing from the beaches, or the rocks and harbour piers. Really exciting is an expedition with the local fishermen out to the richer feeding grounds around the Isle of Man's coastline. Man is the place for record individual catches of the more sought-after fish such as the common skate, cod, mackerel, plaice, and conger eel. Experts recommend the use of heavy tackle and a wire trace for big fish and they say that for congers, inshore fishing at night may be the best bet. The pollack is a fish that travels in shoals in the wake of herring and mackerel and the tope is the British shark fish.

Sea fishing is specially recommended off Douglas Head, Ramsey Queen's Pier, while one of the very best venues is Peel, especially for mackerel. At Port Erin fishing is good in the Bay and from the pier and breakwater. Port St. Mary is the acknowledged centre for boat fishing trips, and from Castletown fishing is good all along the coast. Laxey is an additional centre from which to fish from boats and large catches of whiting are usually obtained.

RIVER FISHING

Almost all the rivers in the Isle of Man are open rivers and permission to fish is usually easy to obtain from farmers and landowners. The Isle of Man Board of Agriculture and Fisheries, 16, Bucks Road, Douglas and Agents in most of the resorts will issue Angling Licences for which modest fees are charged.

The dates for freshwater trout fishing are: 10 March–30 September. Those for freshwater salmon fishing are: 10 March–31 October.

The Freshwater By-laws (1968) forbid the use of a leader trace or cast with a diameter greater than 0·013 inches. It is also illegal to use a gaff or tailer. Maggots are not to be used as bait. Nets only may be used.

Lake Fisheries, Patrick Road, St. John's, consists of a trout farm and catch-out lake from which trout can be caught throughout the year. Permits are not required, but a fee is payable to the owners.

RESERVOIR FISHING
The Clypse and Kerrowdhoo Reservoirs, about four miles from Douglas, are controlled by the Corporation. The Water Department issue fishing permits, either season tickets, ten-day tickets or day tickets. Again the charges are very modest.

Injebreck Reservoir also belongs to the Douglas Corporation. It is situated some six miles from the capital in the West Baldwin Valley. Here spinning is permitted and there is no limit upon the catch taken.

Cringle Reservoir supplies the southern part of the Island with water and comes under the control of the Isle of Man Water Board.

Fishing permits may be obtained upon application to the Secretary's office at 16, Circular Road, Douglas or from the Keeper of the Reservoir.

The restrictions at *all* Reservoirs are as follows:

Residents: Two days per week in any one reservoir.

Visitors: Three days per week in any one reservoir.

Fishing is permitted from 9 a.m. to half an hour after sunset but not later than 10.30 p.m. Wading is forbidden.

PRIVATE FISHING
Douglas and District Angling Club is the only one in the Island to have its own waters. They welcome visitors who may become temporary members for a small fee.

UNDERWATER SWIMMING
Sub-Aqua Sports and Diving enthusiasts are well catered for on the Isle of Man. Because of the mountainous nature of the Manx terrain the coastline is of the kind where a good depth of water for diving is readily accessible from the rocky shore-line without going very far out. Details of the numerous sites are obtainable from the Isle of Man Tourist Board in Victoria Street Douglas and most such points may be approached either by car or public transport facilities, though it is usually necessary to expect a fair amount of walking to reach the shore and diving rocks.

The Isle of Man is ideal for this type of sport. The water is much clearer than is usually the case in British seas which makes for tremendous enjoyment, especially for the under-water photographer. Apart from the fascination and abundance of submarine flora and fauna, there are some absolutely amazing wrecks to be viewed including war-time casualties in the shape of crashed aircraft.

In the deeper waters diving from a boat is the essential method for submarine exploration.

The British Sub Aqua Club has a branch in Douglas and the

Chairman will always be pleased to pass information to keen divers.
The Fire Station at Barrack Street in Douglas supplies compressed
air at standard rates and the Sea Sports Company at Port Erin
is another source of supply as it has a compressor especially for
diving. This is available from mid-May to mid-September.

SWIMMING POOLS
Castletown: Arbory Road
Douglas: The Aquadrome Swimming Pool (and Remedial Baths),
Promenade.
Peel: Marine Parade Pool.
Perwick Bay Hotel: At Port St. Mary.
Onchan: Majestic Lido Pool, King Edward Rd.
Port Erin: Traie Meanaugh Beach.
Ramsey: Queen's Promenade.

DINGHY SAILING
All the Manx ports have good beaches and good launching facilities
to offer visitors who bring their own dinghys to the Island. There
could not be a better way of exploring the beaches, islets and creeks
of the Isle of Man coast than to make your own private cruise along
the shoreline.

At **Ramsey** there is a fine bay, little inshore tide. The launching site
is the Lifeboat slip on the South Promenade. There is a good deal of
local 'handicap' dinghy racing.

Laxey has a smaller, gravelly beach and launching is on the tide
in the harbour or from the beach.

Douglas offers a launch off the slipway by the harbour, or off the
beach.

Castletown beach is a mixture of sand and rocky outcroppings.
Launch in outer harbour or off the beach.

Port St. Mary has the attraction of a concrete slipway to low
water mark, a large dinghy park, and offers a very good cruising area.

Port Erin is a sheltered bay. Launch off its sandy beach.

Peel provides a launch from the lifeboat slip or the beach. The
local races are open to visitors, including the Manx National
Championships. Most clubs sail their 'handicaps' based on
Portsmouth Yardstick so any dinghy is eligible.

YACHTING
A yachting cruise around the shores of Man is one of the most
delightful ways of visiting the Island. You and your boat will be
welcome at any port. At **Ramsey** there are few outlying hazards,
the bottom is mainly sand and the tidal flow is slight. There are three
mooring places by the buoys inside the arm of the Queen's Pier,
and these do not dry out. The entrance to the harbour is quite

straightforward and the Harbour Master's office is on the south side. The favourite berth is in front of the Trafalgar Hotel but the Harbour Master will direct you.

Peel, on the west coast, offers a long outer breakwater where yachts can remain afloat. It extends from St. Patrick's Isle. The Harbour Master's office is on the end of the inner breakwater and the harbour entrance is well-lit and straightforward of approach.

Laxey is a charming tidal port which is also easy of entry. At the harbour top you can moor against the wall in most winds except the easterlies. The Harbour Master may be found in the first house on the right as you approach the village.

Castletown entry is quite straightforward. Sail to the bell buoy which must be left to port and then proceed straight into the tidal harbour which dries out beyond the outer pier. Yachts may be moored in the outer harbour, or on request, the Harbour Master will open the bridge for vessels to be moored almost under the castle walls.

Douglas is the commercial port of Man. There are deep water moorings on the south side of the harbour. The footbridge will be opened on request, for those vessels needing to enter the inner harbour to dry out. The headquarters of the Douglas Motor Boat and Sailing Club are located in St. George's Street.

Port Erin's long narrow bay is sheltered from all but the severe westerlies by its ruined breakwater. There are two large black buoys for mooring between the lifeboat slip and the harbour, which is at the top end of the bay. It is possible to get ashore whatever the tide, at the little jetty near the moorings.

Port St. Mary is a favourite with many yachtsmen. There are visitors' mooring available in the bay and it is possible to lie afloat against the outer breakwater or dry out in the inner habour. There are fresh-water taps on the outer and inner breakwaters. The Isle of Man Yacht Club is located on the right in the High Street of the village, opposite the bank. There are excellent facilities and membership is offered free to visiting yachtsmen.

GOLF

Douglas Municipal Golf Course (18 holes), at Pulrose, one mile from Douglas.

Castletown Golf Links (18-holes), situated on Langness Peninsula to the east of the town.

Onchan Howstrake Golf Club (14 holes).

Peel Golf Course (18-holes), one mile south of the town.

Port St. Mary Municipal Golf Course (9-holes), situated half a mile from the town centre, above the western end of the harbour.

Ramsey Golf Course (18-holes), one mile west of town.

Rowany Golf Course (18-holes), on outskirts of **Port Erin.**

PONY TREKKING

Andreas: Northern Riding School, Willow Lodge, Regaby Road.
Braaid: Grianagh Stables, Ballacallin Beg.
Crosby: Corvalley Riding Centre, Braaid Road.
Douglas: Manx Pony Trekking Centre, 'Highton', Ballanard Road.
Jurby: Mrs. Wallace, Ballamoar Beg, Sandygate.
Michael: Mountain Pony Trekking Centre, Ballakilley Clieu.
Port Erin: Manx Pony Trekking Centre.
Ramsey: J. C. Quayle, North Shore Road.
Sulby: Manx Riding School.
Tromode, Braddan: Jones' Riding School.

BOWLING

Castletown: Off Malew Street, and off The Crofts.
Douglas: Villa Marina, Nobles Park, and Finch Hill (Kensington Road).
Laxey: Glen Road.
Onchan: Onchan Park.
Peel: Marine Parade (adjoining Swimming Pool), and The Headland.
Port Erin: See Port St. Mary.
Port St. Mary: Four Roads (adjoining Railway Station).
Ramsey: Mooragh Park and Walpole Street.
Two Bowling Festivals are held annually, one during the third week in June and the other at the beginning of September. There are valuable cash prizes. Details obtainable from:

> The Bowling Festival Secretary,
> Villa Marina,
> DOUGLAS, Isle of Man.

TENNIS

Castletown: Off Malew Street and off The Crofts.
Douglas: Nobles Park and Finch Hill (Kensington Road).
Laxey: Glen Road.
Onchan: Onchan Park.
Peel: Marine Parade (adjoining Swimming Pool).
Port Erin: Bradda Glen (northern end of Promenade) and Breagle Glen, (off St. Mary's Road).
Port St. Mary: Four Roads (adjoining Railway Station).
Ramsey: Mooragh Park.

Sulby Glen

Horse-drawn tram, Douglas, p. 49

Tail-less Manx cat, p. 15

Elizabethan clock, Castle Rushen, Castletown

The T.T. Races

Section 3   Tourist Trophy and Manx Grand Prix Races

THE T.T. RACES ARE HELD in June and the Manx Grand Prix in September each year. These two events are the highlights of the Manx holiday season and constitute the busiest and most exciting periods in a summer which never lacks interest and enjoyment for anyone and everyone, from the youngest to the oldest.

When the races were first mooted there was a 20-mile per hour speed limit on all English roads and roads could not be closed to traffic for the purpose of racing. Neither of these conditions obtained in the Isle of Man, so the Island became the venue of these two, now world-famous, events.

The first T.T. race was on 28 May 1907, and there were 25 starters, 10 of whom finished the course—the St. John's Course, not the Snaefell Course used today. In the first race the fastest lap was 42·91 m.p.h. Today, on the Snaefell Course, lap speeds of over 100 m.p.h. are common.

The start and finish of the Course is close to Douglas, the total length is 37¾ miles, there are over 200 bends and the highest point is at The Bungalow, near Snaefell Summit.

The following information has been supplied by Shell-Mex-B.P. Ltd., to whom the publishers wish to make due acknowledgment for permission to reproduce it.

"The following notes will be of use to those who wish to watch the racing. They should be used in conjunction with O.S. Map No. 87 and the map of the Circuit which appears on page 35."

Bray Hill (ref. D6)
The bottom of the hill is the most exciting spot, for the machines are at full throttle at this point, the riders needing extra fine judgment on the bend. From the outside of the course, Quarter Bridge, Braddan Bridge and Union Mills can be reached, and from the inside, one can reach Union Mills and the start of the Braddan Bridge S-bends.

Union Mills (ref. C6)
Two miles from the start. This is a downhill fast right-and-left sweep. The best position for the spectator is on the inside of the course, near the exit from the bridge. Nearby vantage points reached from inside the course are Crosby crossroads, Barregarrow (via Baldwin and Brandywell Cottage) and Cronk-ny-Mona.

Ballagarey (ref. C6)
Known to Islanders as Glen Vine corner, this fast bend is about a

B

mile from Union Mills with a downhill approach. This is an excellent point and can be reached on foot from a lane on the outside of the course, 300–400 yds. away. A short ride away are the Crosby crossroads.

Highlander (ref. B6)
A favourite spot with spectators where riders attain very high speeds, reaching 150 m.p.h. before sweeping right and left to the S-bend at Greeba Castle. This latter point can be reached only by detouring through fields and meadows, care being taken as the land is under cultivation.

Ballacraine (ref. A6)
A medium-fast bend 7½ miles from the start where the riders turn north at the start of the tricky Ballig-Glen Helen section. The south-bound road leads to Foxdale, where the Crosby crossroads can be reached. The westerly road leads to St. John's, where a side road branches to Ballig Bridge and another to Laurel Bank and Cronk-y-Voddy.

Ballig Bridge (ref. A6)
Best vantage point is the fast left-hand sweep past the junction leading to Doran's Bend on the approach to Laurel Bank, a right-hander normally treated with respect.

Cronk-y-Voddy (ref. A5)
An undulating straight after the climb up Creg-Wyllis Hill and across open country. At the crossroads Barregarrow, Kirk Michael, Ballig and Ballacraine can be reached.

11th Milestone (ref. A4)
A long, swinging left-hand bend taken at high speed, preceded by two right-hand bends on the drop from Cronk-y-Voddy. This spot has to be reached before the roads are closed and spectators have to remain there until the roads are open.

Handley's Cottage (ref. A4)
Another spot which will tie spectators for the race duration and a short distance from the 11th milestone. This corner, named after the famous T.T. rider, Walter Handley, who crashed there, is a fast S-bend usually taken at over 100 m.p.h.

Baaregarrow (ref. A4)
Shown on the map as Baaregarroo, and, more confusingly, pronounced Bi- (as in bit)-garrow. Despite this it is considered one of the most exciting points for both spectator and rider.
Approaching at full throttle in top gear, the experts take the top bend at about 120 m.p.h. After a slight right kink the riders plummet downhill (a second Bray Hill), to take the left-hander at the bottom—followed by the 13th milestone. Baarregarrow crossroads can be

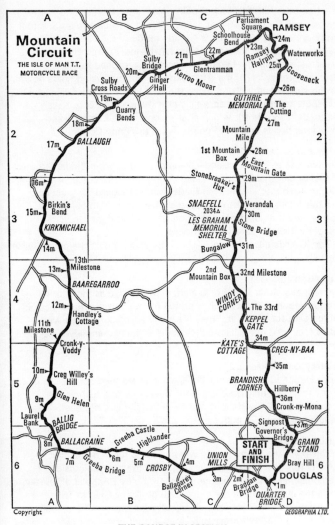

Mountain Circuit

THE ISLE OF MAN T.T.
MOTORCYCLE RACE

RAMSEY

Parliament Square
Schoolhouse Bend
Waterworks — 24m
Ramsey Hairpin — 23m
25m
Gooseneck
26m
21m
22m
Glentramman
Kerroo Mooar
Sulby Bridge
20m
Ginger Hall
Sulby Cross Roads — 19m
Quarry Bends
18m
BALLAUGH
17m
16m
Birkin's Bend — 15m
KIRKMICHAEL
14m
13th Milestone — 13m
BAAREGARROO
12m
Handley's Cottage
11th Milestone
Cronk-y-Voddy
10m
Creg Willey's Hill
Glen Helen
9m
Laurel Bank
BALLIG BRIDGE
BALLACRAINE — 8m
7m
Greeba Bridge — 6m
Greeba Castle
Highlander
5m
CROSBY
4m
UNION MILLS
Ballagarey Corner
3m
Braddan Bridge — 2m
QUARTER BRIDGE
1m

GUTHRIE MEMORIAL
The Cutting
27m
Mountain Mile
1st Mountain Box
28m
East Mountain Gate
Stonebreaker's Hut — 29m
SNAEFELL 2034▲
LES GRAHAM MEMORIAL SHELTER
Verandah
30m
Stone Bridge
Bungalow — 31m
2nd Mountain Box
32nd Milestone
WINDY CORNER
The 33rd
KEPPEL GATE
34m
KATE'S COTTAGE
CREG-NY-BAA
35m
BRANDISH CORNER
Hillberry
36m
Cronk-ny-Mona
Signpost — 37m
Governor's Bridge
GRAND STAND
START AND FINISH
Bray Hill
DOUGLAS

Copyright   *GEOGRAPHIA LTD.*

THE COURSE IN SECTION

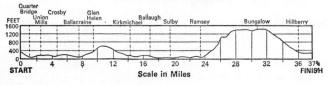

Quarter Bridge · Crosby · Glen Helen · Ballaugh · Bungalow · Hillberry
Union Mills · Ballacraine · Kirkmichael · Sulby · Ramsey

FEET
1600
1200
800
400
0

START   Scale in Miles   **FINISH**

0   4   8   12   16   20   24   28   32   36 37¾

reached from Kirk Michael, Cronk-y-Voddy back roads and from
Brandywell Cottage when roads are closed. It is best to leave motorcycle or car at the crossroads (on the inside of the course). Riders
can be watched at the apex of the left-hander 50 yds. from the
crossroads, while the bend at the bottom is reached from the
Brandywell section of the crossroads by foot, traversing fields down
to the stream and walking along the lane to the bridge. Leaving
transport at the crossroads, a move can be made to Brandywell
Gate (Beinn-y-Phott), which enables one to walk to the 32nd
milestone bends and other points down to Windy Corner.

Rhencullin (ref. A3)
Known also as Birkin's Bend—the spot where Archie Birkin (brother
of racing motorist Tim) was killed during the 1927 practices. His
machine ran into a van when roads were not closed for practices,
but this fatality brought the necessary legislation into being. The
corner, about a mile from Kirk Michael, is a fast right- and left-
hander with a drop down to Bishops Court.

The 'Orrisdale Only' road (outside the course) near the corner leads
to Ballaugh.

Ballaugh (ref. A2)
Pronounced either Billarf or Berlarf, with a bridge as tricky as its
pronunciation, the approach is on full throttle but the hump-backed
bridge calls for first gear. There are many spectacular leaps with
riders facing an immediate right-hand–left-hand manoeuvre, calling
for skilful riding.

Quarry Bends (ref. B2)
Once stationed at the bends the spectators are there for the duration
of the race, but they have excellent views of riding techniques.
Preluding the Sulby straight, the three bends—left, right, left—can
be taken at over 100 m.p.h.

Sulby Crossroads (ref. B1)
At this point the machines are winding up to full song for their high
velocity run down the Sulby Straight. The road on the outside of
the course leads to Sandygate, Ballaugh, Sulby Bridge and Ramsey,
while the inside-course road runs through Sulby Glen to The
Bungalow and the Mountain. A branch road breaks off to wind over
the Claddagh to the Ginger Hall Hotel, a short way past Sulby
Bridge, and a very tricky corner.

Ramsey (ref. D1)
Parliament Square is usually packed with spectators but the corner is
very slow. Further on, May Hill provides a thrilling sweep up to the
Hairpin, a good spot to watch riding styles as the machines start
their climb to the Waterworks Corners.

Gooseneck (ref. D1)
A right-hand bend on a very steep gradient calling for slow negotiation.

Guthrie Memorial (ref. D2)
This name has superseded 'The Cutting', a short way past the Gooseneck, where a memorial to the venerated Jimmy G. stands on the approach to the left-right bends which, through road widening, cause little trouble. From the exit corner riders take to the Mountain Mile, where high speeds are reached on a rising grade.

East Mountain Gate (ref. C2)
A left-hander which has received widening treatment but still calls for care, particularly when mist settles on the mountain.

The Verandah (ref. C3)
An excellent vantage point on the Mountain where the road sweeps through a fast left-hand bend (otherwise known as the Stonebreaker's or Black Hut), from the side of North Barrule to the shelf on the shoulder of Snaefell. There is a valley 800 ft. below. After the entry corner there are four gentle right-hand bends, taken as one sweeping curve at over 100 m.p.h.

The Bungalow (ref. C3)
The old corrugated-iron hotel has now been demolished and its place taken by a brick-built shelter and toilets. This can be reached on the electric railway. Though the building has been removed the trickiness of the medium-fast bend (with the crossing of the railway lines and medium swing through a right-hander) has not been eliminated.

32nd Milestone Bends (ref. C4)
Three left-hand bends taken in one fast sweep and where the experts show their outstanding ability.

Windy Corner (ref. C4)
A medium-fast right-hand bend following a high-speed downhill straight from the 32nd milestone. So called because the wind always blows over the hills from Laxey at this point.

33rd Milestone (ref. C4)
Alterations to the corner have reduced its formidability but it still requires skill to be taken at over 100 m.p.h.

Kate's Cottage (ref. C4)
The Cottage stands on the right-hand side of a fast left-hand bend below Keppel Gate, and its whitewashed face and proportions stand clearly against the mountain background half a mile above Creg-ny-Baa.

Creg-ny-Baa (ref. D5)

Riders travel at high speed from Kate's Cottage, dropping down to this popular point, where they slow from close on 150 m.p.h. to 60 m.p.h.

Brandish Corner (ref. D5)

This medium-fast left-hander midway between Creg and Hillberry calls for great care. It takes its name from T.T. rider Walter Brandish, who crashed there in 1923. This corner is now fenced on the inside, giving a much clearer view to spectators.

Hillberry (ref. D5)

This fast right-hander can be taken at well over 100 m.p.h. as riders roar down from Brandish and climb up to Cronk-ny-Mona. The side road leads to Onchan village where the road alongside the Manx Arms can be taken to Signpost.

Cronk-ny-Mona (ref. D5)

Leading to Signpost Corner on an upgrade, the high-speed left-hand sweep is a good point to study techniques. The road from this point through Willaston Estate was once part of the T.T. Course (from 1911–1914) and Glencrutchery Road is within easy reach.

Signpost (ref. D5)

From Cronk-ny-Mona riders approach at high speed but the corner is a medium-slow right-hander. The slip road to Onchan comes in very useful at times. From Signpost one can reach (on foot) the medium-fast left-hander at Bedstead and the full right, Nook.

Governor's Bridge (ref. D6)

From the Nook the road narrows through the winding approach as riders reduce speed to near walking pace for the acute hairpin. They keep their speed down negotiating 'the dip' before accelerating out through to Glencrutchery Road on their way to the Grandstand.

The Grandstand (ref. D6)

Riders go through at maximum speeds and the scoreboards opposite keep spectators informed of each rider's progress. Overlooking the pits, it is an ideal spot for getting a complete 'picture' and seats may be reserved. There are ample facilities for refreshments and a car-park

OTHER EVENTS

Soon after the celebrated T.T. events comes the International Cycling Week and in July comes the famous 'Southern 100' motor-cycling at Castletown Billown Circuit. Then there is the thrilling International Kart Grand Prix, in Douglas. Scooter enthusiasts are catered for in the Isle of Man Scooter Rally. The Manx Trophy Car Rally is staged in September.

Section 4

Ancient Monuments

FEW PLACES ARE AS RICH as this little Island in the historic monuments of the period of pre-history. It is a period which spans the years from 3000 B.C. to the first few centuries A.D. and on into the eleventh and twelfth centuries. There are many fine monuments dating from the twelfth to the sixteenth centuries but the bulk of them date from the prehistoric periods and those of the Celts and later the Norsemen.

Nearly all the important monuments are mentioned under one of several headings. With so great a number it is possible only to give a bare outline description within these pages but there are many excellent books which provide a great deal of information. One which will help the average visitor is *Ancient and Historic Monuments of the Isle of Man*. It is published by the Manx Museum and National Trust.

CASTLES

BALLACHURRY FORT is an earthwork fort of the Civil War with a moat and four bastions. It is situated about three and a half miles north-west of Ramsey and was erected in 1645 (approximately), for the seventh Earl of Derby

BISHOPS COURT is not strictly a castle but the Bishop's Palace near the village of Kirk Michael. It is believed to have been built by Bishop Simon though very little of his thirteenth century work remains. The medieval tower may date from the fourteenth century but between that time and the nineteenth century many additions and alterations were carried out. Bishops Court has been the home of The Bishops of Sodor and Man since its inception.

CASTLE RUSHEN can claim to be one of the most complete castles in the British Isles for its condition is exceptional. The lower part of the Keep is twelfth century but the rest of the castle proper is thirteenth and fourteenth century. Derby House and the wall known as the 'outer-glacis' are sixteenth century. Castle Rushen was the seat of Government from the tenth to the nineteenth century.

DERBY FORT is a circular fort of stone situated on St. Michael's Island at Castletown. It was built in the sixteenth century, as a defence against the possibility of invasion by the troops of King Henry VIII. During the Civil War it was reconditioned

by the Seventh Earl of Derby, whose initials and the date are
inscribed over the door.

PEEL CASTLE dates from several periods. The Round Tower is
thought to be tenth century but was rebuilt partly with the
crenellated top, which replaced the conical stone roof, an
alteration which took place, probably, in the fifteenth century.
The Castle itself, which no doubt replaced a timber fort,
dates from the middle of the fifteenth century, while the round
fort at the north end of the Island of St. Patrick is very likely
early sixteenth century.

CHURCHES OF THE MEDIEVAL PERIOD

GRAMMAR SCHOOL, CASTLETOWN, was built originally as St.
Mary's Chapel, in the early thirteenth century. Soon after the
dissolution of Rushen Abbey, the Mother Church, two schools
were founded here; they developed, later, into the Academic
College (1669) which, in 1830, became King William's College
and the Castletown Grammar School which continued in these
buildings until 1930. Prior to this there had been a school
housed here since the late sixteenth century. St. Mary's was
the town Church of the Capital until 1698.

LONAN OLD CHURCH was once the Parish Church of Lonan, and
is still used occasionally. This fine old edifice has some signs
of twelfth century work surviving but during alterations the
foundations of a far more ancient church were discovered.
Here may be seen some very fine Crosses of the late Celtic
time. The Church is close to the coast, two miles south of
Baldrine on the Manx Electric Railway.

MAUGHOLD PARISH CHURCH is without doubt, one of the most
important religious sites on the Island. St. Maughold is said
to have landed nearby and founded the Celtic Christian centre
which, since the seventh century has existed here. The present
Church retains still some of the eleventh and twelfth century
work with some slight additions of the thirteenth and fourteenth
century periods. The greatest glory of Maughold is not only
the Maughold Cross but also the many other Crosses kept in
the Cross House near the Church. Here will be found almost
a third of all the Crosses dating from times prior to the Norse
Invasion. Many are fine examples of the work of the period.
There are also some Crosses dating from the several centuries
when the Norsemen ruled in Man, including one which is
thought to be the work of Roolwer, the first Manx Bishop
recorded in history. Outside the Church is the fourteenth
century Maughold Parish Cross, the only one of its kind in
the Island. In superb workmanship it shows four scenes—
Christ on the Cross, The Virgin and Child, the kneeling figure

of a Knight, and a shield displaying a rose with oak leaves.
The Three Legs of Man in the reverse direction to the present
usage, but exactly the same as on the twelfth century Sword
of State, are displayed on the neck of the Cross. Maughold is
on the coast some eight miles north of Laxey or about four
miles south of Ramsey. There are the ruins of three Keills of
the Celtic Christian era in the churchyard.

ST. GERMAN'S CATHEDRAL was and is still, the Cathedral of
Sodor and Man. It is contained within the curtain wall of Peel
Castle. Most of the remains date from the original building
of the early thirteenth century when Bishop Simon was
probably responsible for its construction ; a little earlier work
can still be recognised. This was the finest church on the
Island and the ruins reveal to this day a great deal of beauty
and fine workmanship. It is situated on St. Patrick's Isle at
Peel.

ST. PATRICK'S OF THE ISLE is thought to be of the same period as
the tenth century Round Tower but was rebuilt, probably, in
the twelfth century ; later it was enlarged. The Round Tower
and St. Patrick's Church are the oldest buildings on the Isle
of St. Patrick at Peel.

ST. TRINIAN'S CHAPEL with its ruined and roofless Chapel belonged
once to the Priory of St. Ninian at Whithorn in Galloway.
There was a Chapel here in the twelfth century which was
built upon the site of an earlier Keill. The present Chapel is
undoubtedly fourteenth century and is, in outline a typical
Manx Church of the period. It is near Crosby on the Douglas—
Peel road.

KEILLS OF THE EARLY CHRISTIAN PERIOD

There are a large number of Keills in the Isle of Man which may be of
great interest to the student and historian. Keills are the earliest
known Christian Churches or Chapels ; they date from the seventh
or eighth centuries to the introduction of the modern parish system
in the twelfth century. Most of those which remain are about 16 ft.
by 10 ft. and many have earth walls with a rough facing of stone
on the inside. In a few cases there are remains of altars. Occasionally
there is evidence of the cell in which the cleric lived. The following
are some of the best examples remaining.

BALLADOOLE, ST. MICHAEL'S CHAPEL lies near the western end
of a Celtic Iron Age hill-fort which is situated on a small hill
overlooking the sea. This Keill may be later than some for
mortar has been found in the stonework. If so, it must have
been built on the site of an earlier Church. The site is about
one and a half miles west of Castletown, near Balladoole Farm.

BALLAQUINNEY, ST. PATRICK'S CHAPEL is situated half a mile
south of the Glen Vine corner on the Douglas–Peel road at
Ballaquinney Farm.

BALLAFREER, ST. PATRICK'S CHAPEL is one and a half miles from
Union Mills and about four miles from Douglas, north of the
Douglas–Peel road.

GLENLOUGH, DRUID'S CHAPEL is situated some four miles from
Douglas on the Douglas–Peel road, at Glenlough Farm just
over one mile west of Union Mills.

LAG NY KILLEY means 'The Hollow of the Chapel', and is at the
southern end of the Manx National Trust property at Eary
Cushlin. Three miles of rough walking enable this Chapel to be
reached and details of the route may be obtained either in
Peel or in Port Erin. Further directions are given on page 75.

SPOOYT VANE, ST. PATRICK'S CHAPEL is in Glen Mooar on the
Peel–Kirk Michael road in very beautiful surroundings.

ST. BRIDGET'S CHAPEL is at Eyreton near Crosby on the Douglas–
Peel road. The Keill is on Eyreton Farm half a mile from Crosby.

CROSSES AND HOLY WELLS

About 170 crosses of various types have been found on the Isle of
Man. They date from the seventh to the twelfth centuries and almost
all of these are in the Parish Churches. Drawings and casts of most
of them are housed in the Manx Museum at Douglas.

CHIBBYR Y VASHTEE, WELL OF THE BAPTISM lies 250 yds. north
of the 'Hollow of the Chapel' Keill at Eary Cushlin. For directions
see page 75.

LONAN OLD CHURCH contains some fine Crosses of the Celtic period.

MAUGHOLD PARISH CHURCH. In the Cross House next to this
Church are housed almost one-third of all the pre-Norse
Crosses found on the Island. The finest collection in Man.

ONCHAN PARISH CHURCH in the porch will be seen Celtic Crosses
and one Norse Cross.

ST. MAUGHOLD'S WELL. From Maughold Churchyard make for the
Lighthouse, turn left on to National Trust property and cross
the field to the north side of Maughold Headland, then enter
through a wicket gate.

NORSE PERIOD MONUMENTS

ANDREAS CHURCH. Norse period Crosses include figures representing
Sigurd roasting the Dragon's heart, Odin and the Wolf, and
other scenes from Norse legends.

BRADDAN OLD PARISH CHURCH has Norse Crosses including
one with figures of dragons and Runic inscriptions.

CHAPEL HILL, BALLADOOLE is the site of a Viking Ship Burial,
close by an Iron Age Hill-Fort. For directions see under 'Keills.'

CRONK NY ARREY LHAA is the site of a Burial Mound, possibly
   belonging to the Viking period. It is on Gartfield Farm,
   near Jurby, overlooking the north-western coast.
JURBY PARISH CHURCH. Here there are Norse period Crosses
   and also one or two from the Celtic period. Among the Norse
   Crosses is one with figures depicting Sigurd slaying the
   Dragon. Forty yeards to the north of the Church is a Mound,
   which is probably the site of a Viking Burial.
KNOCK Y DOONEE. Site of a Viking Ship Burial on the summit of a
   hill to the south-east of Knock y Doonee Farm and two and a
   half miles north of Andreas.
KNOCK-Y-DOWAN. Site of a Viking Burial Mound on Ballachrink
   Farm above the Lhen River, near East Jurby.

MONUMENTS OF THE CELTIC IRON AGE

SOUTH BARRULE HILL FORT is known as Manannan's Castle and
   is situated on the summit of South Barrule at 1,585 ft. It is
   the largest and highest hill-fort in the Isle of Man and is best
   approached from the Round Table which is about six miles
   south of Peel.
BALLAKEIGAN is the site of two successive homesteads which were
   still occupied during the first few centuries A.D. It is half a mile
   north-west of Castletown.
BALLANICHOLAS is a small promontory fort with ditch and rampart.
   It is in the upper Santan Valley, near the Garth cross-roads
   between Braaid and Eary.
BALLANORRIS. Like Ballakeigan, this is the site of Iron Age
   homesteads in occupation up to the first few centuries A.D.
   Ballanorris is 100 ft. in diameter and is on Ballanorris Farm,
   about half a mile south of Ballabeg on Laxey Bay.
BRAAID CIRCLE is made up of the stone foundations of three
   successive homesteads of both the Celtic and the Norse types,
   and is situated half a mile east of the Braaid cross roads.
BURROO NED is a promontory fort enclosing the foundations of a
   house. It is on National Trust property close to Spanish Head.
CASHTAL LAJER is the site of a circular homestead, 120 ft. in
   diameter. It is on Cronkould Farm, three quarters of a mile
   south of Ballaugh Village in the Glen.
CASS NY HAWIN is a small promontory fort. A Norse-type long
   house was here as indicated by outline. The site is on a cliff-
   top nearly two miles north of Derbyhaven.
CASTLEWARD HILL FORT is a small promontory fort with a citadel.
   It is situated in the Glass Valley and is two miles north of
   Douglas, near Tromode Village.
CHAPEL HILL, BALLADOOLE is a hill-fort overlooking the sea.
   Nearby there is a Viking Burial site and an early Christian Keill.

The site is near Balladoole Farm which is one and a half
miles west of Castletown.

CLOSE NY CHOLLAGH is a promontory fort with ditch and rampart
on the landward side. Both Iron Age circular houses and a
Norse long house were found here. The site is on the coast two
miles west of Castletown.

CRONK NY MERRIU is a small promontory fort also with ditch and
rampart on the landward side. It is situated on the cliff-top
some 200 yds east of Port Grenaugh.

CRONK SUMARK HILL FORT is a fortified hill-top with two peaks
known as Primrose Hill, half a mile south of Sulby Bridge.

LANGNESS POINT is a promontory fort with ramparts across gullies
overlooking the sea. It is situated one and a half miles walk
from Derbyhaven.

MANANNAN'S CHAIR is the remains of an earthwork which may
be the site of a homestead and is situated near the Staarvey
Road a very ancient route from the Tynwald Hill to Kirk
Michael. The site is one mile from Cronk y Voddy on the St.
John's–Kirk Michael road.

THE BRONZE AGE

ARRAGON MOAR is the site of circular burial mounds on the
Arragon Moar Farm, two miles from the Santan War Memorial.

CRONK NY IRREE LHAA is a burial mound on a 1,500 ft. summit, a
short walk to the south-west from the Round Table.

THE GIANT'S GRAVE is a burial mound cut through by the road
and exposed close to the roadside at St. John's.

THE GIANT'S QUOITING STONE is a very imposing single standing
stone near Ballacreggan corner, Port St. Mary.

THE SPIRAL STONE is a decorated granite boulder situated opposite
Ballaragh Farm between Dhoon and Laxey.

NEOLITHIC PERIOD

BALLAKELLY houses the remains of a megalithic tomb of an unusual
type. It is situated on Ballakelly Farm on the Old Castletown
road, a little over a mile out of Castletown.

CASHTAL YN ARD is a megalithic chambered cairn of the New
Stone Age, about 2000 B.C. It is approximately half a mile
north-east of Glen Mona Halt on the Electric Railway.

KING ORRY'S GRAVE is the largest megalithic cairn in the Isle of
Man. It is situated close to Minorca Station on the Electric
Railway, is a little over a mile from Laxey.

THE MEAYL CIRCLE is a very unusual megalithic tomb of the period
about 2000 B.C. It is set below the summit of Mull Hill to the
north of the village of Cregneish. It is unique in Britain and is
thought by some experts to be unique in the world.

Section 5   Douglas
Douglas to Laxey
Douglas to St. John's

DOUGLAS

Status: Town Borough.

Population: 19,900

Early Closing Day: Thursday.

General Post Office: Regent Street.

Tourist Information Offices: 13, Victoria Street, Sea Terminal.

Places of Worship: Church of England, Methodist, Roman Catholic, Free Churches and other denominations, Salvation Army.

Car Parks: Shaws Brow, Villiers Yard and Chester Street, together with various 'on street' parks.

Cinemas: Regal, Victoria Street, Picture House, Strand Street, The Strand, Strand Street

Parks and Open Spaces: Nobles Park, King George V Park, Douglas Head, Onchan Head.

Local Newspapers: Isle of Man Weekly Times (Tuesday), Isle of Man Examiner (Friday), Isle of Man Courier (Friday), Manx Star (Saturday).

Other Amenities: A great variety of both indoor and outdoor entertainment. Casino open until 5 a.m. Dancing, Concerts, Museum and Art Gallery, Fishing, Golf, Tennis, Bathing, indoor and sea, Boating, Bowls: Aquadrome. Summerland Sports and Leisure Centre.

How to Get There: Services operate from air- and seaports in the U.K. and Eire. See page 8 for further details.

ALL STEAMER SERVICES go to Douglas; the majority of the many passengers arriving at Ronaldsway Airport make first for Douglas, and probably one-third of all visitors travel the Island in a motor-car hired in Douglas. Thus, Douglas, since 1869 the capital and largest township, is quite justly called 'The Gateway to the Isle of Man'.

On an exceptionally clear day, Man is visible from the Mersey

Harbour bar and the first view of Douglas from an incoming
steamer is somewhat unusual in that the long line of blue-and-white
hotels which line the bay appear like cliffs with an occasional dark
patch.

From the Island itself the best view of the capital is from Douglas
Head on the south side of the Bay or from Onchan Head on the north
side. From either of these vantage points the view is a splendid one.
Douglas Bay with its Promenades extends for about two miles in a
half-circle enclosing golden sands with a certain number of rocky
outcroppings.

At the southern end of the Bay one of these outcrops is known as
Conister or St. Mary's Rock. Just below the water-line, the rock was
the cause of many wrecks when small boats and sailing ships ran
for shelter in the harbour during storms. The castellated tower-like
building on this rock, was erected by Sir William Hillary, a Douglas
man, for the protection of any survivors from such wrecks. Called the
'Tower of Refuge', it was built in 1831 shortly after the wreck of the
St. George, when Sir William personally led a successful rescue
party. The same Sir William Hillary had, in 1824, founded the forerunner of the Royal National Lifeboat Institution at Douglas. Sir
Edmund Hillary, one of the conquerors of Mount Everest, is a direct
descendant of this prominent citizen of Douglas.

Immediately behind this magnificent promenade (there are few
with the same kind of splendid sweep), is a first-class shopping area.
The road then climbs the hillside in gentle gradients to reach the
residential area from whence may be obtained fine, expansive views.

For a very considerable distance along the Promenades many
sunken gardens have been laid out. In the season they are always
ablaze with colour, for the Isle of Man enjoys a climate which is
particularly kind to flowers and Manx gardeners are experts at
maintaining a very beautiful show from April through to October.

The Sea Terminal is at the south end of the Promenade. Built to
resemble the 'Three Legs of Mann' this is a fine, useful and ornamental
building which adds a touch of the modern to a town which has
preserved, and rightly so, much from the last century. Beyond it are
the piers and docks, bus and coach station and all the offices
connected with the incoming and outgoing traffic on which the Isle
of Man depends to such a great extent.

In the Terminal Building itself is the Crows Nest Restaurant, its
windows affording views over most of the town. The Jubilee Clock
stands where Victoria Street joins the Promenade from the west. In
Victoria Street the Tourist Information Board on the south side will
be of immense help to visitors requiring information about any part
of the Island. Close by, on the Promenade, is an eight-sided sundial
which came to the Island in 1933 from the Duke of Orleans.

The Villa Marina is situated about one-third of the total distance along the Promenade. This is a complex of very fine gardens, bowling-greens and all the usual seaside attractions including band-performances. There is also an excellent ballroom known as the Royal Hall, which can seat over two thousand. For this reason it is much in demand as a venue for conferences, etc. Opposite the Villa Marina is the War Memorial, an attractive and elegant piece of sculpture which is a credit to the town.

In this neighbourhood is the Isle of Man Holiday Centre chalet complex where there is accommodation for a considerable number of holidaymakers.

THE AQUADROME

The Aquadrome is at the extreme northern end of the Promenade, at the spot known as Derby Castle. This really quite remarkable place consists primarily of two heated sea-water swimming-pools with ample and first-class accommodation for spectators. The larger pool is built to metric standards, the water is heated to 80 degrees and changed completely every three hours. The teaching training pool is shallow, smaller but has the same water temperature as well as a complete change of water every hour. This water-changing system is a very important feature of the place. Inlets are situated every nine inches along the bottom of both pools thus avoiding the alarm sometimes caused by the inrush of a large quantity of water at the shallow end. Excess water leaves the pools by means of over-spill weirs thus preventing the surface of the pool from becoming choppy and turbulent. The air-conditioning system changes the entire atmosphere in the Pool Hall (both pools are in one hall), every fifteen minutes.

The seating accommodation around the pool is adequately heated, while below-the-water-line-vision is provided; further spectator accomodation seats a total of 900 people. A snack-bar, cloakrooms, etc., are provided, while among other services are private baths, showers, Turkish baths, Russian vapour baths, Sauna baths, Scotch and Vichy Douches, a cold plunge, massage and two rest rooms. In addition there are two Aeratone baths for the treatment of arthritis, rheumatism, etc.

The whole complex is built against the bare rock wall of this part of the coast, the open rock face being visible over one end of the Pool Hall.

THE HOUSE OF KEYS

The House of Keys is well worth a visit, especially when the members are sitting. Application should be made to the Enquiry Office in the same building. Even a superficial study of the form of Government and of the historical origins of the present Constitution can be very rewarding.

THE MANX MUSEUM AND ART GALLERY

The Manx Museum and Art Gallery on Crellins Hill is of absorbing
interest. In addition it is particularly useful to those interested in the
history of the Isle of Man. A full size replica of the late medieval
pillar cross from Maughold stands beside the Enquiry Office. The
original dates from the fourteenth or fifteenth century and is the
only one of its kind on the Island.

Among the exhibits which must be seen are the collection of Manx
coins and the skeleton of the Giant Deer, or Irish Elk, which inhabited
north-western Europe at the end of the Ice Age. This particular beast
had disappeared long before there is any evidence of man's presence
on the Island. The archaeology collection includes finds from as long
ago as four or five thousand years B.C. The eighth-century carving
of the Crucifixion, found on the Calf of Man in 1773, is one of the
finest examples in the Museum of this type of work. There is also a
fine collection of Viking remains. Many are authentic, some are
models; all may be said to be of first-class importance. The wonderful
collection of Runic Crosses dating from the years after the Vikings
had abandoned their warlike raids and settled in Man, are shown in
the form of latex casts and photographs, as the originals are still in
the Parish Churches where they were found.

The Map Room and the Natural History Gallery are fine examples
of museum work at its best and should prove of inestimable value
to the student. The centre-piece of the Map Room is a six-inch-to-
the-mile model of the Isle of Man which gives the observer a bird's
eye view of the Kingdom. The Natural History Gallery contains a
Geological section which is of absorbing interest.

No one will wish to miss the Folk Life Galleries which illustrate the
life of the Manx people during the last two centuries. The emphasis
is on country life for agriculture has been always and still is, the
mainstay of life on the Island. The Art Gallery changes its exhibition
from time to time but each one is likely to be of great interest as the
subject is normally and predominantly Manx.

The *Guide to the Manx Museum* which is on sale at the enquiry
desk is a booklet that every visitor should own; it deals with the
exhibits in a much more detailed fashion than is possible within the
pages of this Guide.

ST. GEORGE'S CHURCH

Although Douglas and the Isle of Man have few old buildings of note,
St. George's Church is well worth a visit. It dates from the late
eighteenth century, though its fine square tower gives it a considerably
older appearance. Inside the main gate is the vault containing the
remains of Sir William Hillary, while the Cross which stands alone
marks the mass burial of the cholera victims of 1832–33.

DOUGLAS HEAD

Douglas Head stands right above the harbour, its lighthouse and the hotel with a tower being clearly visible from the town. From the headland there are superb panoramic views to the north and south and also inland as well as out to sea. The hotel tower itself was built long before the hotel, for it was intended as a landmark to help incoming ships. Though there is a bus service out to Douglas Head the distance may easily be accomplished on foot and it makes quite a pleasant expedition to walk there. Afterwards the walk may be extended to continue southwards along the coastal road, the Marine Drive and amid fine rock-girt scenery to Port Soderick, a distance of roughly three miles.

ONCHAN HEAD

Onchan Head is at the north end of Douglas Bay and is yet another point from which to obtain superb views across sea and country. On a clear day the Cumberland Hills in England may be seen to the east. The old village of Onchan is a charming area with a church which was built in the early years of the last century. However, St. Peter's stands upon some of the oldest consecrated ground in the Isle of Man and the present Communion plate, for example, is a fine set from Jacobean times, while among other historical relics interesting Runic Crosses have been uncovered.

The Parish Register at Onchan records the marriage of Captain William Bligh R.N., the remarkable commander of the *Bounty*—the ship in which occurred the memorable mutiny led by another man of Manx descent, Fletcher Christian.

The Horse-drawn Tramway along the Promenade from Derby Castle to the Harbour offers a very pleasant and restful means of retracing the distance of two miles. It provides a delightful reminder of a long-vanished mode of transport—full of nostalgic charm to older people and perhaps dispensing a little novelty to the young!

ONCHAN PARK

This famous playground offers a great variety of amusement and entertainment. It boasts five tennis courts, crown and flat bowling greens, a crazy golf-course as well as an 18-hole miniature course. There is also a boating lake and modern children's playground. The excellent banked cycle-track is a great attraction.

There are Kiddie-cars for the little ones, and miniature racing cars (no licence required) to be hired, while there is nightly Stock-car Racing in the Stadium.

The attractive first-floor restaurant affords diners splendid views out to sea. There are ample safe bathing facilities at Port Jack.

THE MANX ELECTRIC RAILWAY

The Manx Electric Railway which starts at Derby Castle and runs northward to Laxey keeps close to the coast for much of the journey. It is a trip well worth making for the sake of the views over the adjoining countryside and out to sea.

DOUGLAS TO LAXEY

THE SCENERY ON THE JOURNEY from Douglas to Laxey is much the same whether it is made by road or by the Manx Electric Railway but the latter does have two distinct advantages in that the passenger sits considerably higher and in several places the railway runs much nearer to the coast than does the road.

From the terminus at Derby Castle the railway (it was at one time called a tramway and it is still a moot point as to which is the correct term), climbs the hill close beside the cliff-top to Onchan Head. There are lovely views which continue as the track keeps close to the coast as far as the holiday camp and the Glen at Groudle where there is a Halt. Groudle Glen is crossed by the medieval White Bridge and is one of the wooded dells for which the Isle of Man is famous; at the mouth is the tiny Port Groudle.

KIRK LONAN

Between the road and the coast, about a mile north of Port Groudle, is the very ancient Kirk Lonan which stands on ground that has been consecrated for well over a thousand years. It is partially in ruins but services are held there occasionally. Parts of Kirk Lonan are said to date from the fourteenth or fifteenth century.

BEAUTIFUL GLENS

From Kirk Lonan the road and the railway run side by side past innumerable beauty spots and over tiny burns and glens as they strike inland across the blunt nose of Clay Head to join the coast again at Garwick Bay. Here there is another of these lovely Glens. Amid glorious scenery a path leads down the Glen to the coast where two rock passages allow access to the sea and views of Clay Head. The railway and the road follow closely the shore line of Garwick Bay and Laxey Bay to turn inland, crossing the beautiful Laxey Glen by a viaduct to reach the most picturesque and rural of all railway stations. On this short journey the scenery inland is pretty without being spectacular. It is seawards to the north and south along the coast that the visitor discovers the real beauties of this mainly coastal run. It is possible to explore the coast on foot for the whole of this distance but care is needed and the walk should not be attempted by the inexperienced.

THE MOUNTAIN ROAD

The mountain road affords a rather more spectacular journey amid the austere beauties of the higher altitudes. From the seafront at Douglas there are several ways of reaching the A18 route over the hills. This climbs up out of the town almost at once and soon leaves behind the green fields and woods in order to traverse the open moorland.

There are vistas of long valleys and far-off glens set against a background of hills and mountains. From the famous Creg-ny-Baa corner the Laxey road leaves the mountain route to become the B12, which descends gently either to the centre of Laxey Bay and along the coast to the village itself, or through the woods, approaching Laxey Glen to finish close to the railway station. Both routes are delightfully scenic and make for enjoyable driving.

DOUGLAS TO ST. JOHN'S

FROM DOUGLAS THE ROAD ASCENDS quickly affording the visitor fine views as it follows the T.T. Course westwards past Union Mills. This was once a station on the Victorian Railway and is named after the mills which operated here for a very long time. For the whole of this journey the route traverses a depression which carries the River Dhoo, the River Greeba and flowing westward the River Neb. It has been suggested that aeons ago the sea filled this depression, splitting the Island in two. On both sides of the road the hills mainly heather-clad rise in considerable grandeur.

KIRK BRADDAN

About halfway from Douglas to Union Mills lies Kirk Braddan. The new Kirk, consecrated in 1876, is the scene every Sunday morning in summer of an open-air service which many thousands attend. This service is one of the highlights of the summer season. The old Kirk of 1773 has some parts dating from many centuries ago and there is little doubt that this is the site of some far more ancient church. It is a noble structure with a fine tower and an unusual twin bell-cote of a similar type to many found in Northumberland. There was a Synod held here as long ago as 1229 and both inside and outside the church there are many fine Crosses dating from the later Norse settlement. These are known as Runic Crosses and much information about them can be obtained in the Manx Museum at Douglas. This old church, its protecting trees and not too far distant hills make a fine picture and a remarkably interesting study.

From Kirk Braddan the road follows closely the River Dhoo with Greeba, 1,383 ft., on the north side, largely covered with conifers. Among a small plantation of copper beeches is Greeba Castle, once the home of Sir Hall Caine, the Manx novelist.

ST. TRINIAN'S

The next point of interest is St. Trinian's Church on the north side of the road. Although the present Church is probably fourteenth century, it is quite certain that one or more ancient churches preceded this one. The original name was St. Ninian and it was built, definitely upon the site of a Keill. In 1780 Marown Church was built on the south side of Crosby and much material from St. Trinian's was used for this purpose. Today the latter building is roofless and if one believes the old legend it has been always.

According to the story an evil spirit called a 'buggane', blew the roof off as fast as it was erected; every time the workmen re-erected it the 'buggane', with a mighty blast, blew it away. It was suggested that if a tailor could cut out and make a pair of breeches in less time than it took to devastate the roof then this calamity would not recur. The village tailor collected all the necessary cloth, needles etc., and sitting in the chancel commenced work. He ran out of thread at the last button and quickly left the Church to fetch more. As he returned the 'buggane' arrived and with another mighty blast blew away the roof and the tailor, who was never seen again! No further efforts were made to roof St. Trinian's and it has, therefore remained in its present state for hundreds of years. So much for the legend! In about 1230 the Church of St. Trinian's and that of St. Ronan

Braddan Old Kirk

(Marown) were allocated to the Abbey of St. Ninian at Whithorn in Galloway. Both were of course, earlier buildings than the present ones.

ST. JOHN'S AND TYNWALD HILL

A little over a mile further along the route is the most historic if not the most ancient site in the Isle of Man. St. John's Church and Tynwald Hill probaly owe their position to the crossroads which occur a little to the east. Here the valley of the River Neb crosses the Valley of the Greeba River and doubtless, since time began, there have been track crossings here. Every 5 July the Church of St. John the Baptist sees the gathering of the Members of the House of Keys and of the Legislative Council for a meeting of the Tynwald Court. The significance of the date is that this was old Midsummer Day and was the occasion when the ancient Scandinavians held a 'Thing' or general meeting to proclaim their laws to all the people. Although the date of the first 'Thing' is lost to historians it is assumed that it was early in the Viking occupation of the Isle of Man. Until the fourteenth and fifteenth centuries these meetings, or 'Things', were held in various other places on the Island but since then St. John's has become the official venue of 'Tynwald Day'.

After a preliminary service in the church a procession, arranged in preordained order, leaves the building to follow the gravel path which leads to the hill. First, four sergeants of police head the march and they are followed by Coroners of the six Sheadings and the High Bailiff. Seventeen Captains of Parishes representing all Man fall in behind the Mayor of Douglas and the Chairmen of the Commissioners of the principal local authorities. After them walks the Vicar-General, followed by the Clergy, who are said to represent the part once played by the priests of the Scandinavian god Thor. Behind the Vicar-General there follows the Speaker and the members of the House of Keys. The members of the Legislative Council follow the Keys and in due turn they are followed by the Attorney General, the Deemsters and the Lord Bishop. Behind the Bishop the Sword-Bearer carries the ceremonial Sword of State and the Lieutenant-Governor completes the procession—his presence representing the interest of the reigning monarch in the proceedings.

When the procession has passed along the rush-strewn path and reached the Hill of Tynwald due order is observed. The Lieutenant-Governor climbs to the top platform to where two chairs are placed for himself, representing the ruler, and for the Bishop, the spiritual ruler. Around them the Legislative Council, including the 'Deemsters' or men of law, form a phalanx, while on the middle-slopes are the members of the House of Keys. The ceremony of 'Fencing the Court' then takes place. This is the declaiming of an ancient form of words calling upon those present to witness the fact that the Court is fenced. There is then a resigning of office by 'Coroners' from the various electoral divisions of the Island and a bestowing upon new 'Coroners' their Wands of Office, and the ceremony of 'Swearing them in'. Then the laws passed by the Legislature since the last meeting on Tynwald Hill are read out to the Assembly in both Manx and English. Tynwald Day is a Bank Holiday and National celebration in the Island and at one time every family tried to ensure that at least one of its number attended the ceremony. Today it is a novelty which attracts visitors and has otherwise become an observance among only the most conscientious Manxmen. There was more excitement about the Tynwald Meeting in 1945 when, for the first time, the reigning king (the late George VI), was present in person in his capacity as Lord of Man.

Beside the path to Tynwald Hill is the great Celtic Cross of granite which is the Manx National War Memorial.

SIDE ROADS THROUGH THE HILLS

Along the way on roads such as the A23, A22 and A21, out of Douglas, there are several attractive side roads penetrating into the hills towards the north and west. These invite exploration either by the walker or the motorist and afford opportunities for gentle excursions inland. One route is along the valley of the East Baldwin River which may be followed for some five miles to just beyond the hamlet of Ballachrink where it becomes a hill track. A mile further westwards is the B22 road which keeps close to the West Baldwin River, passes through the larch and pine trees of the Colden Plantation just beyond the Reservoir and eventually joins the B10 road before it bears northward to Kirk Michael.

The countryside is here most reminiscent of Exmoor for it abounds in rolling moorland, woodland plantations and trout streams. Indeed the West Baldwin route in particular passes between Colden summit (1,599 ft. high), to the west, and the Carraghan peak (1,640 ft.) to the east. Both heights are just a little lower than Dunkery Beacon on Exmoor and as with most moorland country the air is fresh even on the hottest days.

Section 6

Laxey
Laxey to Snaefell
Laxey to Ramsey

LAXEY

Status: Village.

Population: 1,250

Early Closing Day: Thursday.

General Post Office: New Road.

Places of Worship: Church of England, Methodist

Parking Places: Captain's Hill, Promenade, Dumbell's Row

Parks and Open Spaces: Laxey Glen Gardens, Forestry Board.

Other Amenities: Bathing, Dancing, Sandy Beach, Glorious Gardens, Camping site: industrial archaeological trail.

How to Get There: (*By Rail*). Electric tramway from Douglas. (*By Road*). Bus or coach from Douglas.

LAXEY'S UNIQUE TOPOGRAPHY contributes considerably to its charm. The upper town with its country inns, shops, cafés and expanding residential area has evolved around the main highway between Douglas and Ramsey. The lower town nestles beside the sea and sand and still has much picturesque, old-world charm from the days when it was mainly a fishing port. Today there are only a few fishing-boats in the harbour, one or two coastal vessels call, and the yachts of sailing enthusiasts are anchored there. An attractive Promenade flanks the bay and the beach is claimed to be the safest on the Island. The two parts of the resort are linked by the Glen Road with its upper stretch known as Captain's Hill.

The disused lead mines have provided the basis for the ornamental gardens which are such a feature of the route through the Glen. The Laxey River flows through gardens and rock-pools down to the sea, past houses set at different levels along the valley.

There are one or two light industries around Laxey but they do not introduce anything like a heavy industrial atmosphere. There are mainly small light industries, a flour mill which has been in business for at least a hundred years (indeed, it is the only one on the Island), and there is, in addition a woollen mill which has also a pleasant shop attached in which hand-woven woollen goods are on sale. These items are very popular with visitors.

To the north of the Glen lies Laxey Head and plenty of rock-girt coast for those who enjoy rock-scrambling.

Half-way up the Glen is the station of the Manx Electric Railway which connects the resort with Douglas to the south. The 'station' will be a pleasant surprise to those who see it for the first time. It has a most pleasantly rural aspect, for the booking office is embowered in trees and shrubberies and there are rustic seats for the travellers to use.

Just near it, amid the trees, is the Parish Church.

THE WATER WHEEL

The 'Lady Isabella' Water Wheel is situated about half a mile above the station. It is over a hundred years old and ceased working only when the lead mines gave out. This is the largest such wheel in the world and is, in many ways, quite remarkable. It was designed by a Manxman, Robert Casement, and the following description is taken from the Official Guide issued by the Laxey Village Commissioners.

'The "Lady Isabella" has a diameter of 72 ft. 6 in., a breadth of 6 ft. and a circumference of 217 ft. Its top speed was two revolutions a minute and it raised 250 gallons of water a minute from a depth of 300 fathoms. The water to supply the wheel was brought from reservoirs in the mountains and ascended through a circular white pillar to the top of the wheel.'

The purpose of this famous 'Wheel' was to pump the lead mines free from water but now that the mines are no longer operating, the Lady Isabella' remains a masterpiece of engineering and is a considerable showpiece, attracting thousands of visitors. The climb up the 96 steps to the platform of the tower is well worth the effort for the sake of the glorious views over the Glen and out to sea. Westward there is a splendid panorama across the moors to Snaefell.

CENTRE FOR EXPLORATION

One of the greatest attractions of Laxey is the verdant countryside. Trees are everywhere and luxuriant shrubberies flourish. Flowers bloom for eight months of the year and from the terraced walks and natural vantage points there are fresh and beautiful views. In addition, it is an excellent centre from which to explore the countryside which includes the surrounding hills, the rolling moorland and Snaefell which is, at 2,034 ft., the highest point on the Isle of Man.

LAXEY TO SNAEFELL

THE MANX ELECTRIC RAILWAY, Snaefell branch, will carry less active visitors to within yards of the summit of Snaefell, by a very fine and scenic route providing many good and extensive views. For the fit and energetic, however, to walk is the only right and proper way to ascend any mountain the height of Snaefell.

There are two routes apart from crossing the open moorland itself. One is the track on the north side of Laxey Glen which starts at the site of the 'Great Wheel'. It then climbs steadily alongside the Glen to the disused mines a quarter of a mile from the Mountain Road and a mile north of The Bungalow.

The other is the road from Laxey to Baldhoon from where a footpath climbs the mountain to The Bungalow. From The Bungalow the railway may be followed. A shorter route lies through the wicket gate just north of the railway line and follows a plain footpath to the summit. Here the Summit Hotel supplies refreshments. From The Bungalow the distance is barely one mile; from Laxey it is about five miles.

SIX KINGDOMS

From the summit of Snaefell there are truly magnificent panoramic views, and on a clear day it is popularly held that six Kingdoms can be seen. These are (1) The Isle of Man, of which almost the whole is visible, spread out below; (2) The Mull of Galloway in Scotland; (3) Cumberland in England; (4) Wales; (5) Ireland, and, if you look upwards, the Kingdom of Heaven! Sometimes the mountain summit is lost in mist and cloud so that the views are blotted out. But it is worth waiting for a clear day and then indeed, the opportunity to survey the surrounding countryside and the distant prospects should not be missed. The walk from Laxey is bracing but not particularly difficult, while the continually varied views are most rewarding.

The Bungalow is the highest point on Mountain Road. It is also a stop on the Snaefell Railway as well as a vantage point on the T.T. race course. Here there are three roads, the Mountain Road itself, which comes up from the south, continues northwards and then gently downhill, with the long ridge of North Barrule, 1,860 ft. on the eastern side. To the west are the lesser heights and the very beautiful Glen Auldyn as the road leads, finally, almost into Ramsey itself.

HIGH MOORLAND

North-westwards from The Bungalow is the glorious road passing through the wooded length of Sulby Glen where the route follows closely the course of the River Sulby. This is one of the most delightful runs in the Isle of Man and is especially recommended for car touring. On reaching the flatter terrain at the foot of the moors the visitor may turn right for Ramsey or left for Kirk Michael and Peel.

Three quarters of a mile south from The Bungalow and striking westwards, is the third road; rather narrower but still good. For some distance it follows the 1,300 ft. contour-line before dropping down gently through the high hills to a junction where once more the choice may be made—right for Kirk Michael left for Peel. All three of these roads afford the visitor an opportunity to explore some of the finest expanses of the high moorland country including the more secluded glens. The higher reaches of these areas also provide numerous vantage points from which to enjoy superb views across the Island, and in many instances beyond the coastline, over the sea to neighbouring shores.

FOR THE WALKER

Rolling moorland and hill-country is exactly the terrain which offers the dedicated walker certain advantages not enjoyed by the motorist. The most solitary glens, the loveliest mountain streams, high barrows and stone circles are often accessible only to the determined explorer on foot. This is especially true of the country north of the Douglas—Peel main road where with the aid of map and a stout stick the traveller may 'wander lonely as a cloud' all day.

LAXEY TO RAMSEY

BETWEEN LAXEY AND RAMSEY neither the road nor the railway follow the coast as closely as on the southern half of the journey from Douglas. Both follow the Glen on leaving Laxey although at a greater height, thus affording the traveller some very fine views.

When within a few hundred yards of the coast, which here is rock-bound and very picturesque, both road and railway turn north along the coast to the Halt at Bulgham Bay. Within a mile there is a further stop at Dhoon Glen which is open to the public and has a footpath to the sea at Dhoon Bay. The Glen is advertised by the Railway Company in glowing terms but in fact, the terms of the advertisement are, if anything, an understatement of the charms of Glen Dhoon as will be readily acknowledged after visiting one of the most peaceful and lovely coastal glens in the Island.

Beyond Dhoon the railway and the coast road turn inland, keeping roughly to the same contour line across the lower hills which, however, afterwards rise more steeply on the landward side. The next halt is Glen Mona where a narrow road runs the length of the wooded valley to Port Cornaa, where the Ballaglass River enters the sea in as tight a little cove as one could ever imagine. The whole of this coast, from Douglas to Ramsey is made up of rocky cliffs with innumerable small bays and sandy coves not always easy of access. But experienced walkers and climbers may well find it enjoyable to scramble over the rocks and explore the cliff tracks which hug the coastline.

Within a further two miles the railway leaves the road and stops at two points at the head of Ballaglass Glen where there is a footpath through the woods down to the sea. A new feature here is the interesting Ballaglass Nature Trail.

The Mona and Ballaglass Glens are connected by a narrow lane along which it is possible for the motorist to drive so that both these valleys may be easily visited. The main road, after leaving the railway, continues north for two miles then turns south-east once more to rejoin the railway track at the most northerly of the two Ballaglass Halts. From here they continue contiguously to within half a mile of the rocky coastline. In this part of the Island there are many tiny lanes and tracks which lead down to the shoreline at some lesser-known places.

MAUGHOLD HEAD AND THE VIEW

There is another halt near the deep bay known as Port Mooar and here the railway and a side road cut north-west across Maughold Head while the main road passes within a few hundred yards of the headland itself. This is, for many reasons, a place which no visitor should miss. The view from the Head, below which there is a lighthouse, is truly magnificent and on a clear day the Point of Ayre to the north and Clay Head to the south are both in view together with some miles of the rugged, picturesque coast. A part of this outstanding headland belongs to the Manx National Trust.

ST. MAUGHOLD VILLAGE

The tiny village of Maughold is an ancient place with roots in the far distant past. St. Patrick has always been accepted as the Patron Saint of the Isle of Man and St. Maughold has been venerated always as next in order of sanctity. He, it was, who is said to have been cast ashore on the nearby headland and that where he knelt and thanked God for his deliverance from the sea, a spring of water welled up. At that spot he built a Keill, destined to become a place of pilgrimage, and doubtless he lived nearby. Other Keills were built and possibly other buildings so that the site of Kirk Maughold was to Manxmen from the fifth century onwards, a place of great sanctity. Within the present churchyard, which corresponds, probably, to the area occupied by the original Priory, are the remains of three Keills which may be viewed by visitors. These all date from the seventh and ninth centuries. The Church itself stands upon the site of a fourth Keill.

THE CROSS HOUSE

In the Cross House on the right hand side of the gate is a collection of Celtic and Norse Crosses together with an explanatory note. These are in the care of the Manx Museum and Ancient Monuments Trustees, from whom more information may be obtained. Many of these Crosses were found in the churchyard and many more within the Parish, suggesting that Kirk Maughold was at one time the probable centre of Celtic and Norse Christianity in the Isle of Man. The oldest parts of the Church are said to be eleventh century although alterations over the succeeding centuries have changed the original plan. A leaflet is obtainable in the Church which gives in greater detail the history of this very ancient place.

THE PARISH CROSS

The Parish Cross stands beside the gate but was originally outside it. It dates from the fourteenth century and is the only one of its kind in the Isle. It depicts in fine workmanship the Virgin and Child, the kneeling figure of a Knight and a Shield displaying a rose with oak leaves. On the neck of the Cross the Three legs of Man are displayed in reverse direction but exactly the same as on the Sword of State dated as twelfth century. There are many other points of interest and beauty that should be seen ; those with a love of the best from the past should not miss this lovely little Church or the Cross House.

A WALKER'S PARADISE

From Maughold Head the coast quickly loses its ruggedness as it descends to the glorious sands of Ramsey Bay at the southern end of which there is another Halt. It will have been noticed that, if the visitor is travelling by the Electric Railway there are few, if any, points of interest that cannot be reached easily from the nearest railway Halt. The great square of country enclosed by the Laxey–Snaefell line, The Bungalow–Ramsey road and the coast is truly a walker's paradise. It includes all the lovely glens running down to the shoreline, the many heights and sweeps of moorland on the landward side, and lastly North Barrule with its long ridge keeping almost the same altitude all the way to the Mountain Road near The Bungalow. It is, certainly, a countryside to lure the traveller afoot.

✳   ✳   ✳

RAMSEY

Status: Town.

Population: 5,500

Early Closing Days: Wednesday and Thursday.

General Post Office: Court Row.

Places of Worship: Church of England, Methodist, Roman Catholic, Salvation Army, Free Church, Seamen's Bethel.

Parking Places: Market Place, Mooragh Park, College Street, Station Road.

Parks and Open Spaces: Mooragh Park, Vollan Flats.

Local Newspapers: Isle of Man Courier and Isle of Main Examiner (Friday).

Other Amenities: Bathing, Dancing, Golf, Miniature Golf, Putting, Bowls, Boating, Motor boats, Yachting, Canoeing, Tennis.

How to Get There: Bus or coach from Douglas. Electric Railway during summer.

APART FROM DOUGLAS, the capital, Ramsey is perhaps the most modern of the holiday resorts in the Isle of Man and is well-served by buses.

Ramsey is the centre-piece of, though it is not in the centre of, the curve of Ramsey Bay with its great sweep of sand and shingle from Gob ny rona to Shellag Point and beyond. The town is often called Royal Ramsey because of an unscheduled visit in 1847, by Queen Victoria and the Prince Consort. This occasion is commemorated by the tower known as the Albert Tower which is on a hill a little to the south of the town. Ramsey Bay is very well sheltered and this aspect of it makes for safe sea-bathing—an added attraction for thousands of visitors. Indeed, the Bay is often sought as a shelter by vessels caught in the storms which beset this stretch of the coast. Ramsey Lifeboat is a very famous one and in its many years of service has saved some 500 lives.

THE HARBOUR AND THE SULBY RIVER

From the Harbour with its twin piers and lighthouses, The Queen's Promenade extends as far as The Queen's Pier which is built out into the blue waters of the bay for a distance of half a mile. The town has two natural divisions made by the Harbour and the Sulby River. The river, joined by the Auldyn just outside the town, flows through the resort and via the Harbour into the sea. The two portions are connected by bridges.

Ramsey Harbour is tidal, and is much in use by fishing and coastal vessels as well as by pleasure yachts. South of the Queen's Pier another safe bathing beach runs under the Ballure Mount Promenade and extends nearly to the cliffs of Gob ny rona. Fishing is perhaps, more popular in and around Ramsey than elsewhere in the Isle of Man. The Sulby River is nearly all free fishing and is, in addition the largest river in the Island. Sea fishing is also very popular at Ramsey and there are plenty of facilities for hiring tackle and rowing or sailing boats.

THE TOWN

Ramsey itself is a very pleasant resort set at the foot of the hills with splendid open views to the south, looking towards North Barrule, Snaefell and the windswept uplands in the centre of the Island. To the north there are vistas of fine sand and shingle set against the flatter, lusher grasslands towards Point of Ayre.

There is a smart shopping centre in Ramsey and in the attractive Mooragh Park is a lake shaded by fine Palm trees which testify to the justice of the town's claim to have the sunniest and the most equable climate in the Island. The forty acres of Mooragh Park together with the lake, provide facilities for considerable amusement; there are tennis-courts, bowling-greens, miniature-golf and putting, and on the lake, sailing, rowing, canoeing and motor-boating.

THE PROMENADE

Ramsey is a great centre for all kinds of water-sports and regattas and water-pageants are a noted feature of the season. At the western end of the town is a first-class Golf Links of 18-holes where visitors are very welcome to play.

There are few ancient buildings. The oldest is Ballure Church, dedicated to St. Catherine and built in 1637. The site on which it stands was itself a very ancient burial-ground and probably there was a Keill there although no sign of it now exists.

As with all the popular resorts in the Isle of Man, the walker may make Ramsey his headquarters for some truly glorious exploratory expeditions. The course of the Sulby river through its Glen is one attractive feature; to the south lie moors and the peaks while northwards there is a fascinating vista of sand, sea and meadow stretching away to Point of Ayre. This is excellent walking country, easy on the legs and rewarding to the eye.

NORTH OF THE SULBY RIVER

Starting from the Ballure Glen, just south of Ramsey, the flat lands sweep northwards in an almost level plain and westwards to the coast at Gob ny Creggan in something approaching a half-circle along the base of the hills. For a third of this distance the Sulby River marks the course of this break in the formation of the land mass and for the whole distance the main road to Kirk Michael and Peel follows the same natural course. In consequence this is a picturesque route to travel with hills close up on one side and the spreading, level plain upon the other.

THE NORTHERN PLAIN

All over the northern plain there are roads and field tracks, lonely hamlets and very many farms. By the Sulby River the land is rich and fertile but these qualities deteriorate further north. Here there is an area of low hills interspersed with rough, boggy land—at one time quite probably a lake, or lakes.

On the west side, north of Ballaugh, there is an area of fenland—the home of many wading birds, an irresistible terrain for the botanist and nature-lover. To balance this, the northern tract has also some good agricultural land and this too has an air and an atmosphere of its own. It is a land of space and soft horizons, pastoral calm and long, light vistas and its almost Arcadian peace is both rewarding and enriching after the noise and confusion of city life.

Laxey

THE NORTHERN COAST

To walk round the coast of the northern plain of the Isle of Man is to
experience solitude; one might walk the whole distance from Ramsey
to Kirk Michael, some twenty-two miles, without meeting a single
other person. Sea-birds flock here and so do many land-birds,
especially the waders. Though in places the sandbanks are steep,
this is virtually a flat, sandy shore making for fine, easy walking
and except along the northernmost stretch one is never too far from a
house or farm. The road also stays quite close to the sea.

On a calm day when tiny breakers come in, endlessly swishing
and rippling over the flat sands, the whole aura is one of such peace
as few of us are able to enjoy, though we may dream of doing so.

At the Point of Ayre there are two lighthouses and a fog siren;
one light is set at a height of 106 ft., while the lower light at a
height of 33 ft. is set close to the water's edge. The siren sounds
three low-pitched blasts every minute-and-a-half.

Nearby, in this area there is a sand-blown stretch of wilderness
where tiny wild flowers and patches of gorse and broom flourish
amid crops of rough bogweed. This part of the Island is certainly a
walker's paradise and provides a striking change from the mountains
and moorlands.

RAMSEY TO PEEL

IN MANY RESPECTS this road is the most picturesque in the
Island. Two distinct types of scenery dominate almost all of its
length; to the south lie the hills and open moorland while to the
north lies the agricultural plain merging into the sea.

GLEN AULDYN

Westwards out of Ramsey the A3 road hugs the wooded hillside
between the Sulby River and the lower slopes of the Snaefell
heights. The valleys cutting into these hills in the north are many,
varied and beautiful. The most notable is Glen Auldyn about a mile
out of Ramsey, where there is a motor road as far as the village. A
rough track follows the burn for a further two miles. Numerous side
streams feed the main river, sparkling among the rocks and stones
and splashing down in pretty waterfalls in the more secluded places.
The water-courses make useful, if sometimes rough tracks to the
hilltops.

MUTINY ON THE BOUNTY

At the foot of Glen Auldyn, to the east of the water, is Milntown,
the ancient home of the Christian family who have played always a

The 'Lady Isabella' Water Wheel at Laxey

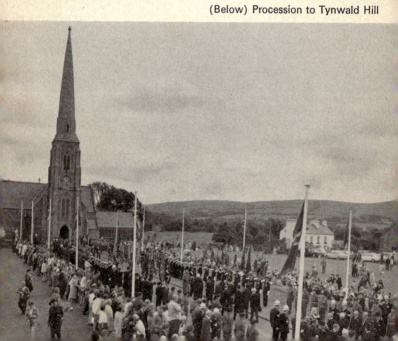

(Above) Speaker reading the laws

Tynwald Ceremony, pp. 53, 54

(Below) Procession to Tynwald Hill

Peel Viking Festival   p. 73

Cregneash, p. 80

St. Patrick's Isle, p. 70

prominent part in the life of the Isle of Man. The most famed descendant is, of course, Fletcher Christian, who led the mutiny against Captain Bligh, Master of the *Bounty*, in 1790. The mutineers afterwards established a colony on Pitcairn Island.

To the west of the Glen is Sky Hill, scene of the great battle of 1079 which established the rule of Godred Crovan, later known to history as King Orry. This Norse chief had, in fact, ruled in Man earlier and been exiled by Malcolm, King of Scotland, his overlord. After one unsuccessful attempt four years earlier he regained for himself, in 1079, the crown of Man and ruled very successfully for the next sixteen years.

A stony track and footpath leads from the main road at the foot of Sky Hill up over the rising moorland to the Mountain Road at the very start of the Glen Auldyn under the summit of Snaefell.

SULBY GLEN

The short but attractive Glentramman and Glenduff are passed before Sulby Bridge is reached. Here the road crosses the Sulby where that very beautiful river bears eastwards in its course to flow down to Ramsey and the sea. It is the longest and largest of the Manx rivers and its valley is one of the most rugged and wild among the Glens.

There are several hotels close to the mouth of the Glen and a very good motor road traverses the length of the valley up to The Bungalow on the Mountain Road. This run encompasses some of the best of the wild, woodland scenery of Sulby, as well as the open moors under Snaefell summit and presents remarkable views from varying angles and heights.

CURRAGHS WILDLIFE PARK

A mile before the village of Ballaugh, westwards from Sulby Bridge is the Curraghs Wildlife Park, established in 1964. It is a remarkable achievement for so small a nation as Man and is rightly one of the most popular attractions in the Island. Some 60,000 visitors tour the Park each year.

The Nature Reserve has been set up on some 211 acres of the Ballaugh Curraghs of which 26 acres have been developed as a Wildlife Park. The Park is not only very attractive but it contains many kinds of birds and animals from all over the world. Among the more exotic are the flamingoes, penguins, llamas, monkeys and a puma. Among the more colourful birds are white-cheeked, red-crested and purple-crested touracos, parakeets, barbary doves and golden and silver pheasants. In the same paddock as the Australian wallaby is the Loghtan sheep of Man of which there are only a very few remaining today. The male of this species has four long, curved horns and the female only two which are somewhat shorter. There are many more animals and birds which can be viewed in comfort

c

amid the finest surroundings. A café provides refreshments, and buses and coaches take visitors right to the gates. This Nature Reserve is a place of absorbing interest to both botanists and naturalists because much of the area it occupies was still marshland and little explored.

The village of Ballaugh is picturesque and, reputedly prosperous. The name is said to derive from 'Balla', a town and 'lough', a lake. The old Church of Ballaugh stands a little north of the village, on the site of one or more very ancient predecessors and the first known Rector was recorded in 1408, while the oldest register in the Island, dated 1598, belongs to this church. Within a mile of the church the site of a Viking burial was excavated in 1946.

GLEN DHOO

The village stands at the foot of Glen Dhoo, which, though not as picturesque as the Sulby Glen, nevertheless makes an attractive car excursion. The road, admittedly a narrow one, climbs to the open moors below Slieau Dhoo, skirts the plantations and then bears southwards to join the road which links The Bungalow route (B10) with the main road to Kirk Michael. The road climbs to a height of 1,000 ft. just below Slieau Dhoo, with Slieau Freoaghane and Sartfell to the west, Snaefell to the east, affording magnificent views across rivers and glens stretching away in all directions.

BISHOPS COURT

After Ballaugh the road bears southwards and the northern plain narrows to a strip, soon to blend with the sea as the line of the hills slope down almost to the water's edge south of Kirk Michael. In this narrowing strip stands Bishops Court, which would appear to be, in its oldest parts, contemporary in age with Castle Rushen, i.e. thirteenth century. The oldest surviving part of Bishops Court is the tower now called King Orry's Tower. The reason for this is not known though it is thought that the tower was once part of a fortress guarding the north–south road. This seems a reasonable supposition for its position, just where the gap between sea and hills widens out, would be the most suitable place for a defensive structure. In addition its walls are, in places, 12 ft. thick and it seems likely that so massive a structure would have been for defence purposes.

Bishops Court seems have to have been mentioned first in the early thirteenth century, under the name 'Balicure', as being in the possession of the Bishops. In the same document is mentioned Knockcrogher which means Gallows Hill. This is thought to be Cronk y crogher, a small hill nearby. The Bishops had, in those days, like English barons, rights of life and death over the populace and held courts to determine such sentences. In fact there was a gibbet on their land at

Cronk-e-coghee and the crypt of the Cathedral housed a prison for offenders. No other British Bishop had such summary powers.

The present Bishops Court consists of the Tower, the dwelling-house and the Chapel. These three portions were built at different times over the centuries and the last major reconstruction was the work of Bishop Powys in 1860. Perhaps the greatest benefactor of all was Bishop Wilson who took office in 1698 and repaired and extended the then ruined Court, carrying out in addition some fine landscape gardening. The Chapel is used today as the Island Cathedral pending the possible restoration of St. German's Cathedral at Peel; the base of the Tower is still used, after seven or eight hundred years as the meeting place for the Manx Convocation.

BISHOP'S GLEN

Opposite Bishops Court is the Bishop's Glen, another of those charming wooded valleys which enable the walker to climb up through the most pleasant surroundings to the moors and the open hilltops. in this case Slieau Curn, 1,153 ft. high, from whence with careful map reading a great many summits may be reached without much arduous climbing.

Bishops Court

KIRK MICHAEL

Kirk Michael, less than two miles south of Bishops Court is the largest village in the north-west of the Isle of Man. It is a very peaceful, pleasant, though small resort and being only a short walk from the sea the excellent beaches and firm sands are popular with bathers. There are many attractive walks in the neighbourhood, particularly for the hill-walker who can explore a dozen prominent heights including Snaefell all within a day's outing. The plain but interesting Parish Church has a fine collection of Runic and other Celtic Crosses.

From Kirk Michael there are two roads south; one follows the coast closely, the other travels about two miles inland to St. John's from where a right turn leads to Peel or a left turn to Douglas. Immediately south of Kirk Michael is Glen Wyllin which follows the west side of the St. John's road for some two miles and then where it passes under the main road, the water comes tumbling steeply down from the narrow gap between Slieau Freoaghane and Sartfell, another grand ascent for the walker.

GLEN MOOAR

Glen Mooar (Michael) is situated a little less than a mile from the road and should not be missed. In this Glen is one of the highest waterfalls in the Isle of Man—'The White Spout' or Spooyt Vane— easily accessible despite its lonely setting. In Spring this Glen is a riot of primroses and is very lovely at any season. Since at no point does the route climb above four or five hundred feet it is an easy expedition to accomplish.

Among the trees there are the ruins of a Keill in a very pleasant and peaceful spot. One mile along the St. John's road from Kirk Michael is the tiny hillock known as Cronk Urleigh where a Tynwald meeting was held for the one and only occasion in about 1422.

GLEN HELEN

Those who travel the St. Johns' road have one other charming Glen to explore before the downhill run to Peel. This is Glen Helen, fed by three streams, one from Slieau Maggle, one from Colden and one from Slieau Ruy (1,570 ft.), and part of the great central 'backbone' of the Island.

The lower reaches of this enchantingly pretty Glen afford an easy journey to the traveller on foot. Before proceeding on the main route to Peel choose a suitable viewpoint and look westwards across the coast of the Isle of Man to the Mountains of Mourne in Co. Down, N. Ireland. To the south lies the great rift which splits the Island virtually into two and the road beside the River Neb brings the traveller the remaining three or four miles down into Peel.

PEEL

Status: Town.

Population: 3,300

Early Closing Day: Thursday.

General Post Office: Market Place.

Places of Worship: Church of England, Methodist, Roman Catholic, Salvation Army, Grace Baptist Church, Plymouth Brethren.

Parking Places: Derby Road, Douglas Street, Market Place, Christian Street, Marine Parade.

Parks and Open Spaces: Creg Malin Park.

Local Newspaper: Peel City Guardian (Friday).

Other Amenities: Swimming, safe sea bathing and open-air pool. Fishing, Golf, Boating, Tennis, Dancing, Bowls, Camping Site.

How to Get There: (*By Road*). Bus or coach from Douglas.

WHILE THE ENERGETIC TOWN COMMISSIONERS have done great work in modernising Peel and have provided almost all that the holidaymaker could ask for, it remains attractive mainly because of the natural beauties of its situation and the age-old inherent charm of the town and the port, for these are the magnets which draw the visitors each year.

Peel is near the northern end of a stretch of coastline which, for rugged beauty is hard to beat. Rocky, broken and endlessly indented, the western coast of the Island is variedly beautiful from some five miles north of Peel right down to Spanish Head in the south. Inland the town affords easy access to really delightful country, and good roads abound to aid exploration. Indeed, the countryside both to the north and south of the great cleft which runs in a fairly straight line between Peel and Douglas, offers some exceptionally fine hill walks which may be long and arduous or easy and attractive as individual tastes require.

North of the cleft are the highest hills and the wilder, rolling moorlands, while to the south lie the gentler hills and softer grasslands with woods and valleys intermingling to a much greater extent.

THE TOWN

Of Peel itself, suffice it to say that a visitor who does not enjoy this
town must be very hard to please. It has all the quaintness of narrow,
winding streets, around its ancient harbour but it boasts also a good
shopping centre, a fine camping park and a handsome Marine Parade.
Thistle Head and the cliffs to the north supply much quiet enjoyment
and glorious panoramic views; St. Patrick's Isle with Peel Castle
and St. German's Cathedral offer a different, but just as important
source of pleasure to those interested in architecture and history.

THE PORT OF THE ISLAND

In Manx–Celtic, Peel should be Purt-ny-Hinshey or the Port of the
Island; there is little doubt that before Douglas modernised her
harbour that is what Peel most certainly was, for it has a natural
harbour with fishing and trading activities with origins going back
through many, many centuries. It has lost much of its importance
as a trading port but it is still the fishing port of the Island. Many
parts of Peel are modern today but it would be a great loss if the
antique charm of old streets and fisher cottages, small alleys and
byways were demolished to make way for more concrete and
stainless steel!

THE PARISH CHURCHES

The present Parish Church is dedicated to St. Germain while the
former Parish Church of St. Peter has been pulled down to be
replaced with a Garden of Rest. There is, however, the old tower
surviving and this houses the clock presented by a Manx exile living
in Canada.

ST. PATRICK'S ISLE

St. Patrick's Isle is the centrepiece of Peel. On its small area of some
7½ acres there is the ruined Cathedral of St. German, and the famous
Castle. These two contain within their ancient stones much of the
history of Peel.

The natural harbour and St. Patrick's Isle are the chief contributors
to Peel's long historic importance in the annals of Man. Most of
the acreage of St. Patrick's is taken up by the mass of the Castle,
inside the walls of which lie the ruins of the Cathedral of St. German,
the Church of St. Patrick and the Round Tower; other buildings
were attached to the Cathedral. It seems probable that from earliest
times there has been a defensive structure of some kind on the island.
Flint implements have been found.

Of the present buildings which are falling sadly into ruin, the
oldest appears to be St. Patrick's Church though it is almost
certainly not the first church to stand upon this site. St. Patrick's

was the Parish Church of Kirk Patrick, while for some reason not now apparent, there was also a Parish of St. German, with the common boundary running right across the island.

This state of affairs could not have been particularly convenient for in those days there was no roadway to the Isle, so the Parish Church of St. Peter's was built on the mainland to serve both St. Patrick's and St. German's Parishes. This it did until replaced by the present Parish Church of St. Germain.

It would seem that St. Patrick's dates from about the eleventh century but the Round Tower which is part of the Church, may be older. The whole undoubtedly replaced a church that was in existence as long ago as the fifth century. Today, St. Patrick's is sadly in need of repair but much of the beauty of the original architecture remains. Alongside the Church is the building known as The Armoury, probably seventeenth century.

THE WALL AND THE GATE TOWER

The red sandstone wall which completely encircles this Islet is of much greater interest; although it is of various dates, the oldest part between the gatehouse and the Cathedral is almost certainly of the same period as the gate-tower and the gateway entrance, both built about 1350. Inside the walls is a 'defence mound' now grass covered, added probably at the same time as the final portion of the wall— thought to have been completed by the Stanleys in 1500 or thereabouts.

THE CATHEDRAL OF ST. GERMAN

The Cathedral Church of St. German, named after the saint who was a nephew of St. Patrick, is the noblest and most beautiful of all the remains on St. Patrick's Isle and it is still the Diocesan Cathedral Church of Sodor and Man.

Possibly in the fifth century, a keill was built by St. Patrick or his followers and in the early twelfth century this was replaced by a very beautiful little church which forms today the chancel of the Cathedral. Certainly the oldest part is the chancel, then the tower and transepts, followed by the nave. Various dates have been allotted to these several portions but it does appear most likely that the early twelfth century saw the beginning, at least, of the later Cathedral.

Although the tower, transepts and nave are not at all in keeping with the original chancel, they make, nevertheless, a fitting and glorious church. Several centuries have been spent in the building of the Cathedral and at every stage the same red sandstone has been used, thus giving the most beautiful effects now that time has mellowed and softened the once vivid colouring. The nave has a south arcade which is probably the most fascinating of these ruins; there was no north arcade. The Cathedral is very small by English standards but it is not less beautiful, nor the workmanship less fine for that.

THE BISHOP'S PALACE AND THE GIANT'S GRAVE

Just to the north of the Cathedral are the remains of the Palace of the Bishops. Only the Banqueting Hall is of note. It seems uncertain whether the Bishops ever did use the Palace, for Bishops Court has been their home for many centuries. Within the confines of the Palace is a well whose water is wonderfully clear; another freshwater well exists near the Sally-Port. Further along the north wall is the Warwick Tower, thought to have got its name because the Earl of Warwick was imprisoned there. However, this is not well substantiated though Richard II did banish the then Earl of Warwick to the Isle of Man, for that Earl, Thomas Beauchamp, was only in Man for one year before being returned to the Tower of London. During his stay 'Warwick Tower' was not completely constructed and it seems improbable that Sir William Scrope, who was paid very lavishly for the care of his prisoner, would have lodged him there.

Nearby is the Giant's Grave. The origin of the 'Grave' is unknown and since the mound measures 90 ft. by 5 ft. it is not surprising that a very good story has grown up as to the origin of the occupant. The giant is said to have had three legs thus, naturally, he was a Manxman, who annoyed everybody by jumping from hill to hill throwing huge boulders all over the place. He threw one lump of quartz weighing many tons against the hillside in Lhergydhoo where it broke into several pieces. These pieces may be seen still, about two miles north of Peel. Finally, St. Patrick gave the giant such a cursing that he jumped over the headland known as Contrary Head into the sea. He was later discovered in his grave where he has remained ever since!

CORRIN'S TOWER

Fenella's Tower near the western Sally-Port is mentioned in Scott's 'Peveril of the Peak' while across Fenella's Beach is Peel Hill from whence may be had a first-rate view of the Isle, the Cathedral and Castle, with the open seas beyond. A mile or so south of Peel Hill and on the same long ridge is Contrary Head and Corrin's Tower from where may be seen magnificent views of the west coast of the Isle of Man; it is a steep climb but the panoramic views are most rewarding.

Corrin who built the Tower, was a non-conformist who demonstrated that one could be buried in other than consecrated ground by having the bodies of his wife and children transferred from St. Patrick's churchyard to a spot marked by two small obelisks, close to the tower, and he himself was later buried nearby. Fifty feet in height and standing upon the 500-hundred ft. contour the Tower now belongs to the Corrin Trust. Regarded locally as a 'folly' the Tower is, nevertheless, a useful landmark.

CLIFF WALKS

The cliff-top walks, both north and south of the town are among the many glorious expeditions which can be made from Peel. These walks take in some of the finest coastal scenery to be found in the Isle of Man. Glen Maye is yet another of the delightful Glens for which the Island is so justly famous. It contains a very fine waterfall close to the Waterfall Hotel. The Glen may be entered from the village of Glenmaye or from the coastal approaches, and whichever way is selected the visitor will discover one of the loveliest of beautiful wooded glens ever to open upon a fine stretch of coast. Glen Mooar (Patrick) is a deep valley between the coast and the north-west flanks of South Barrule; again the best entrance is from the village of Glenmaye.

Another method of seeing the very fine coastal scenery to advantage is from the sea. Weather permitting, boat trips may be made north or south of Peel. This way, many of the fascinating caves (some of which are unapproachable from the land), can be seen as well as the rock-bound shoreline.

A VIKING RAID

In July each year a very colourful ceremony and probably the only one of its kind in the British Isles, takes place. The original landing and sacking of Peel which happened in A.D. 798, is re-enacted by local men dressed in Viking costume. They land from a number of Longships which are an exact replica of the Longships of 1,200 years ago. This is an occasion on which much fun is engendered and it certainly makes a never-to-be-forgotten day, especially for children.

FISHING

Peel is the fishing port of the Island and in this connection there is much of interest to be seen. Trips can be made with the local fishermen, and the famous kippering-plant should be seen as well as the freezing-plant for scallops and prawns. Both these plants are modern and contribute considerably to the export trade. In the season a great many Scottish and Irish herring boats fish out of Peel and trips can be arranged in these boats which are often out at night; a night at sea in a small boat can be a very interesting and enjoyable experience for the townsman.

Peel has a reputation for being the best fishing ground for amateur or professional in the British Isles. From the breakwater or from small boats in the Bay, many fine catches have been made, while inland there is first-class trout-fishing from most of the streams, even from many of the smaller ones.

C*

GAELS AND NORSEMEN

It is said, often, that there is a big difference between the Manxmen who live to the north and those who live south of the Douglas–Peel geological cleft; in the north of the Island there is said to be a preponderance of the Gael, while in the south the Norse or Viking blood and character predominates. If this is correct then Peel will no doubt show this difference in character and blood to a greater extent than other places in the Island, for Peel is, in many ways, the Viking City. It was the first stronghold of these pirate-adventurers who became, later the colonists and thereafter contributed so much to the life and culture of the Isle of Man.

PEEL TO PORT ERIN

NEARLY THREE MILES INLAND from Peel is the historic St. John's, a pretty village and a good centre for the walker who wants to be near the base of the hills which are both north and south of that great cleft in which St. John's sits so comfortably.

THE BATTLE OF SANDWAT

Many believe that the Battle of Sandwat, fought in 1098 between the peoples of the north and the south of the Island, took place on the terrain between Peel and St. John's. From this battle, perhaps, originated the view that there is a significant difference between the two. It is related that the women of the south gave invaluable assistance to their menfolk in this battle and that in return they were awarded certain rights of property that were never enjoyed by the women of the north

From St. John's the road which follows the valley can be taken to reach Douglas. It is a pleasant road which starts among the high hills and runs gradually into less hilly country where agriculture dominates and the plantations are seen less frequently. Here the walker needs to keep to the footpaths and the little lanes which are, in any case, very pleasant. The railway also followed this valley from Douglas to Peel and to the lead mines at Foxdale. This line closed some years ago but it must have been a very attractive route.

THE WITCHES HILL

Southwards from St. John's the road lies beside a stream and the route of the now abandoned railway to the village of Foxdald. This is a grand little run of about three miles, starting with the very steep height of Slieau Whallian, sometimes known as 'The Witches Hill'. This is because of an old legend which asserts that suspected witches were rolled down the slope of Slieau Whallian in barrels studded with spikes on the inside. If they arrived at the bottom alive they were regarded as proven witches (for the Devil had protected his own) and promptly killed. If they were dead on arrival then there was no further argument! This tale is so much a part of the folk-legends of Europe generally that it forces one to speculate upon the fact that even the loneliest islands were not cut off from the mysterious power of old folk-lore traditions. Any reader who remembers Grimms' Fairy Tales will recognise the spiked-barrel-trial for witches and evil-doers.

FOXDALE
On the east side of Foxdale are the now disused lead mines which first brought the need for a railway to this pretty village on the banks of a tributary of the River Neb. It is from the Hamilton Fall at Lower Foxdale that the village takes its name. It comes from the Scandinavian 'Foss' for waterfall and 'Dal' for valley, which through the centuries has become 'Foxdale'. Certainly it has nothing to do with foxes for they are entirely unknown in the Isle of Man.

The Foxdale lead mines have an interesting history. They were first opened up in the early eighteenth century and soon produced quantities of lead with a high silver content. During the later years of the eighteenth and the whole of the nineteenth centuries these mines grew in importance. The railway from Douglas arrived at Foxdale in 1886 and this was, of course, a major event to the fast-growing and very busy village. However, before long the prosperity of the mines began to wane, and in 1911 the last closed and some twenty-five years later the railway closed also.

SOUTH BARRULE
Three-quarters of a mile south of Foxdale, in the midst of a plantation, a side road, the A36, turns right, or west to climb the northern flanks of South Barrule to the Round Table, an ancient Burial Mound that awaits excavation, and then over one of the most scenic of routes to Port Erin and Port St. Mary. The walk from the crossroads at the Round Table to the summit of South Barrule is quite short. From the summit there are some exceptionally fine views.

EARY CUSHLIN, MANX NATIONAL TRUST
A mile and a half south of the Round Table on A36, a narrow side road leads off to the north-west and the Manx National Trust Estate of Eary Cushlin, acquired in 1958 and open to the public. It consists of some of the finest, though not the highest, hill scenery in the island, with a stretch of coastline second to none. It extends from the plantation north of Eary Cushlin to the western slopes of Cronk ny Arrey Laa. A rough track leads from Eary Cushlin southwards for about a mile to Lag ny Killey which means the Hollow of the Chapel: here the ruins of the most remote Keill and the cell in which the first incumbent lived among the lonely moorland scenery and close to the wild and broken western cliff can still be seen.

A right turn at the Round Table will take the visitor on to the A27 road and south-west for three quarters of a mile to the village of Dalby. A road leads directly to Niarbyl Point from where some great views of the coast southwards to Bradda Head can be seen. This view includes Niarbyl Bay, the western edge of the Manx National Trust Estate of Eary Cushlin, The Stacks and Fleshwick Bay, a very fine stretch of coast. Two miles north of Dalby is the village of Glenmaye and the entrance to the Glen of Maye. The remaining three miles to Peel is by a pleasant road which passes the village of Patrick.

TO PORT ERIN

The A36 southwards from the Round Table is a mountain road with great attractions. The route embraces several heights and ever-changing views amid fine scenery. It is a road that should not be missed. An alternative route to Port Erin lies through Colby by taking the left turn at the Round Table on A27. Though very pretty this road is not, perhaps, so spectacular as the mountain road. From the latter road through Colby there are many side roads and lanes which lead the visitor to hillsides and glens which are not so crowded as the more popular and better known beauty spots. Six miles south of the Round Table by the mountain road, and Port Erin is reached; the same journey is a mile or two longer via Colby.

Port Erin

PORT ERIN

Status: Village.

Population: 2,580

Early Closing Day: Thursday.

General Post Office: Church Road.

Places of Worship: Church of England, Methodist, Roman Catholic.

Parking Places: Promenade, Shore Road, Station Road.

Erin Arts Centre: Victoria Square.

Parks and Open Spaces: Athol Park, The Glen, Bradda Glen.

Other Amenities: Bathing, safe and excellent for children, Boating, rowing or motor boats, Dancing, Fishing, Golf, Tennis, Open Air Swimming Pool.

How to Get There: (*By Rail*). Summer only service from Douglas by Isle of Man Railway. (*By Road*). Bus or coach from Douglas.

THIS ONE-TIME FISHING VILLAGE has grown into a very delightful resort and is the centre of some of the finest scenery in an island which lacks little of scenic beauty. Port Erin has not allowed modern trends to stifle its natural and time-honoured beauties. It is in most things the antithesis of Douglas and for the lover of peace, solitude and natural beauty it stands alone. The village cannot be seen until one is almost upon the outskirts, for it is screened by low hills on the landward side, by the mighty Bradda Head to the north and the almost equally prominent Mull Hill to the south. Though it retains its old-world charm it can still offer the visitor good shops and all those amenities necessary to a quiet but very pleasant holiday.

SWIMMING

It is, perhaps, as a bathing place that Port Erin really outdoes its neighbours. Here the beach is safe, shallow enough for those who do not like deep water, yet deep water is a very short distance out, making it an almost perfect bathing beach. At the northern end of the village and the beach is the open-air swimming pool which is built into the rock at the foot of Bradda Head; the Manx name of this pool is Traie Meanagh Bath. Just around the corner is Spaldrick Bay, a tiny bay with a beach, which is often more solitary than the larger, more popular sands of the main Bay.

AQUARIUM

The Marine Biological Station and Aquarium is on the south side of the Bay, beyond the Lifeboat House. This is a place of absorbing interest where research into marine life is carried out and the fish hatchery breeds and releases into the sea some millions of plaice and the larvae of the lobster in large quantities. The Aquarium and Fish Hatchery are open to the public, and the whole project is controlled by the University of Liverpool.

KIRK CHRIST RUSHEN

Both Port Erin and Port St. Mary, about a mile and a half to the south-east, are in the Parish of Rushen and share a common Parish Church, generally known as the Kirk Christ Rushen. It stands about a mile from both places and is close to the site of a very ancient Celtic Church. It was made the Parish Church some 700 years ago and was partially rebuilt and enlarged in the later years of the eighteenth century. This is an extremely interesting little church and has a list of Vicars which gives the name of eacn incumbent since 1574.

BRADDA HEAD AND MILNER'S TOWER

The Tower on Bradda Head known as Milner's Tower was, to quote the inscription over the door 'erected by public subscription to William Milner, in grateful acknowledgment of his many charities to Port Erin and of his never-tiring efforts for the benefit of the Manx fishermen'. The walk to this Tower should be undertaken by everyone for the views from the Head are exceptionally beautiful while the nearer prospect of the cliffs themselves, rising to about 400 ft. against Bradda Hill a little northwards at an altitude of 700 ft., is most facinating. A footpath runs to the Tower from the north end of the Promenade.

PORT ST. MARY

Status: Village.

Population: 1,508

Early Closing Day: Thursday.

General Post Office: Bay View Road.

Places of Worship: Church of England, Methodist.

Parking Places: Promenade, off Bay View Road.

Other Amenities: Golf, Dancing, Concerts, Bowls, Bathing, Yachting, Boating, Fishing.

How to Get There: (*By Rail*). Summer only service from Douglas by Isle of Man Railway. (*By Road*). Bus or Coach from Douglas.

IN MANX-GAELIC the name is Purt Noo Moirrey or 'The Harbour of Mary' and it is said to be named after The Virgin Mary by some very early Celtic missionaries who landed in this sheltered bay. They also built a small Keill which is now beneath the Town Hall but is remembered in the name Chapel Beach.

Built of locally quarried limestone the village is situated in graceful style around the harbour; the streets and houses, many of them quite old, mount the very gentle hillside and make a superb picture as seen from the sea. But despite the fact that Port St. Mary has cherished much that is old and dignified from its past, it supplies also all the main ingredients of a modern holiday. The shopping area is very good as in all the Manx resorts and in addition the sporting facilities, especially for boating and yachting, are excellent.

SMUGGLERS
At one time this village was concerned solely with fishing. A certain amount is still undertaken, but, like all the old-time fishing ports, it has suffered from the competition of the larger boats and the increasing commercialisation of the trade. Today, visitors are the chief concern of the villagers. In some respects Port St. Mary is slightly reminiscent of the small ports of Galloway in south-west Scotland and it is a fact that many years ago there was a close liaison between the smugglers of Port St. Mary and those of Kirkcudbright. This is commemorated in Kirkcudbright by the naming of Manxmen's Lake. Today, when Port St. Mary is the headquarters of the Isle of Man Yacht Club, the Mull of Galloway, sixteen miles away is a natural objective for sailing runs. Yachting and boating generally are favourite sports in Port. St. Mary.

TWO BAYS
There are officially, two bays in Port St. Mary; Chapel Bay and the Bay of Rocks. Chapel Bay is in fact only the inner recess of the Port St. Mary Bay and possesses fine, clean sands which children can enjoy. Separated by the Gansey Point from Chapel Bay is Bay ny Carricky or the Bay of Rocks. The word Gansey is supposed to derive from a Norse word meaning Magic Point. Today the magic is due to its sunny situation and the lovely view of the village and the hills behind.

Southwards and separated from it by the southernmost part of the village as well as a wide promontory which contains the golf links, there is Perwick Bay, a delightful rock-girt cove with grassy hills sloping down nearly to the water's edge.

THE LITTLE PEOPLE
Two other activities for which Port St. Mary is well known are concerts of Manx folk-songs and displays of dancing in traditional

costume. If there are any stories of the 'Little People' to be heard, it is in Port St. Mary that one will hear them, for although the Isle of Man generally still asserts its belief in the 'Little People', it is in Port St. Mary and this southern tip of the Island that the assertion appears to find fertile soil in which the belief may survive. In such a friendly place it is quite easy to believe in these 'small folk'—especially the 'mooinjer-ny-gione-veggey'—the 'good little people'.

THE HARBOUR

The harbour is a picturesque place, not now so busy with fishing boats although still retaining its kippering house. However, in the holiday season, with scores of yachts and smaller boats for which Port St. Mary is quite a famous and very safe harbour, there is much activity. There are two piers and breakwaters. The most southerly was the last to be built and it affords ample protection from all states of the weather and the tide. The shorter and more northerly was erected in 1812. Each has a beacon. A rather unusual coastal pathway on raised piles allows easy access to the harbour from where boating excursions to the remarkably broken and indented coast between Port St. Mary and Spanish Head can be made. Opposite the harbour entrance, in the middle of the Bay ny Carricky and marked by a beacon is the Carrick Rock. Between the harbour and Perwick Bay is Kallow Point from where a view may be had towards Castletown and Castletown Bay to the east.

The small peninsula south-west of Port Erin and Port St. Mary is served by only one road yet it contains some first-class scenery.

NATIONAL TRUST VILLAGE AND MUSEUM

The road runs from Port St. Mary to Spanish Head and is barely three miles long; it passes between the Mull Hill and Cronk ny Arrey and is throughout an attractive route through pleasant scenery. The first place of interest is the village of Cregneash which is the property of the Manx Museum and National Trust. Here there is an open-air Manx Folk Museum of very great interest. It consists of the Weaver's House, Karran Farmstead, Turner's Shop and Harry Kelly's Cottage. These are open to the public.

The idea of the Museum is to show and preserve some parts of the life of the Manx countryman that has now disappeared for ever. The houses and other things seen were commonplace less than 100 years ago, in fact, before the last war, many such country cottages, smithys, etc., were still in being. Harry Kelly's Cottage is about 150 years of age and is a fine example of the crofters cottage of the last century and earlier. The Karran Farmstead is typical of the crofts of former days. These buildings and about thirty acres of land would be about the usual size. All the buildings were thatched.

The handloom in the Weaver's House is the last in the Parish and it would be difficult now to find an operator. The Turner's Shed was a joiner's workshop and still houses his lathe and tools, etc. The Smithy is a good example of the Blacksmith's workshop of days not long gone by.

All four of these sections of the Museum are well worth a visit. Here during the summer may be found a small flock of the Manx Loghtan Sheep.

SPANISH HEAD

The village of Cregneash is situated at the 450 ft. contour-level and looks out over the gently sloping hills to the Spanish Head, the Calf of Man and the open sea. Spanish Head came by its name through the story of a galleon of the Spanish Armada which was said to have been wrecked here, though most historians discount this as pure fiction since every one of those unwieldy ships is said to have been accounted for in other places. The Head is a delightful spot from where there is a clear view of the Calf of Man. It is a lonely and bracing spot peopled by sea birds and the ghosts of Manxmen who have sailed the seas to other lands.

From the end of the A31 to the Head itself along the cliff-top is about a mile and makes a very delightful walk which may be continued eastwards and then northwards to Port St. Mary. The total distance is less than four miles along the cliffs and has some

Sugar Loaf Rock

very fine coastal scenery; more than half of this walk is within the bounds of the land owned by the Manx National Trust. This area of outstanding scenery starts at the end of the A31 and covers the coast southwards to Spanish Head and then a mile further west. On nearing Port St. Mary look out for the area known as 'The Chasms' and be very careful, for this little region is pitted with cracks and potholes, many buried beneath the long grass or other herbage. It is a fascinating place but care is needed.

Immediately south of Perwick Bay is the Noggin Head or Kione y Ghoggan, a sheer cliff with some remarkable strata clearly visible on the 200-ft. face of the rock. A little farther south is the Sugar Loaf, a detached rock with the height of about 100 ft. Along this stretch of coast there are a number of caves which can be visited by boat only.

THE CALF OF MAN

From the end of the A31 a track leads down to Calf Sound, the narrow channel between the mainland and the Calf; in the channel is the island of Kitterland and one or two smaller islets. The tide races through the Sound with fearful force, especially when there is a strong wind from the south-west and an incoming tide.

The Calf of Man is a Bird Sanctuary and the property of the Manx National Trust. In the summer, weather permitting, the Calf may be visited by boat from Port St. Mary. There are two Wardens in residence during the summer and they operate a private post office from which special stamps can be purchased. The Calf covers about 600 acres and the highest point is over 400 ft. On the south-west point, at The Stack, a remarkable pillar of rock 100 ft. above the waves, are the two lighthouses built last century, and nearby is a modern lighthouse which has replaced the one built on Chicken Rock. This stands about a mile out to sea, south-west of The Calf.

The Calf is famous for its seabirds, and scores of thousands nest there. These visitors from afar make the Calf, throughout the seasons, a delight to the naturalist. The chough is one of the species, which, though rare in England, can be seen in hundreds on the Calf. The Chicken Rock' gets its name, apparently, from the numbers of 'Mother Carey's Chickens' (or Stormy Petrels) which frequent the Rock when, at low tide only, it is above the water.

✳   ✳   ✳

CASTLETOWN

Status: Town.

Population: 2,820.

Early Closing Day: Thursday.

General Post Office: Castle Street

Tourist Information Office: Town Hall, Parliament Square.

Places of Worship: Church of England, Methodist, Roman Catholic.

Parking Places: Farrants Way, The Parade, Parliament Square, Shore Road.

Parks and Open Spaces: Poulsom Park.

Other Amenities: Tennis, Golf, Bowls, Bathing.

How to Get There: (*By Rail*). Summer only service from Douglas by Isle of Man Railway. (*By Road*). Bus or Coach from Douglas.

FOR MANY CENTURIES, Castletown was the capital of the Isle of Man and the site of the finest castle; today it remains one of the outstanding towns of this Island. Small by comparison with Douglas, Castletown has an intensely interesting history and much lovely country within a short distance.

Castletown remained the capital of Man until 1862 when the Government transferred to Douglas. To the inhabitants of Castletown it is still the capital and always will be! In many ways the town retains the aspects which belong to a bustling seat of government as well as the romantic aura emanating from magnificently preserved Castle Rushen—that splendid symbol of Castletown's official status in bygone days.

With its famous King William's College, former Grammar School, and Old Parliament House, Castletown is rightly tenacious of its claim to be a centre of learning and justice. Its conservative charms are such as to give it a special appeal to the visitor.

CASTLE RUSHEN
The reason for the choice of Castletown as the site of the Castle and seat of Government is not especially clear but it may have been dictated by the topography of the surrounding countryside. The

inland area was, most probably, in ancient times, the only really good agricultural territory under cultivation, for the bulk of the Isle of Man, then as now, consisted of rolling hill-country. In consequence invaders would covet this richer farmland and so make this part of the coast their main target. Obviously there was great need for stout defence, and so the Kings of Man set about the task of building the massive structure which, after numerous phases of reconstruction, stands today looking still as solidly defensive of the town as it was in the turbulent past.

Originally the sea washed right up against the Castle walls on the east side where there was a very shallow harbour since filled in, partly by natural silting up and partly in order to provide the basis for the road which today affords an easy approach. To the south and west were the open sea and the wide shingle beach while only from the north was there a road and this a narrow one between two lakes, the present Malew Road.

On consideration it is clear that the Castle builders chose the site very well and this is borne out by the fact that only twice in history has the Castle fallen to an enemy.

Of all the many castles in the British Isles there is not one that has weathered so well as Rushen. It might have been built yesterday for it stands as square and solid as it did in the thirteenth century, its limestone walls but little defaced by time. The history of any fort or defensive structure which may have stood there before the present

Castle Rushen

one is simply not known. Undoubtedly there was some such construction but any remains are now below the three distinct sections of Castle Rushen.

These three sections were built in or earlier than the thirteenth, fourteenth, fifteenth and sixteenth centuries. It is difficult to date any of these quite remarkable buildings, history being very uncertain on this score. The whole Castle is constructed of the native limestone which was quarried, most probably, from the nearby Scarlett Quarries. It has outlasted the centuries better than many another type of stone.

The first structure was the original Keep, the basis of the present central tower; then came the side towers, three in number and the curtain wall with the portcullis gateway. Later an outer wall was built on the east side and earth walls to the west and north. There are other buildings such as Derby House, residence of the Lords of Man, ruins of the chapel, the dungeons and a Court Room which is used still for the Deemster's and Magistrate's Courts today.

In the course of its long history the Castle has been used as a fortress, a barracks and military storehouse, a prison, a lunatic asylum, residence for the Governor, and also as a Court of Justice, which last function it still serves as mentioned above. The Keep, the first core of the fortress stands exactly as it did when first built, though surrounded by much later structures. The single-handed clock in the south tower is reputed to have been given by Elizabeth Tudor, and her gold monogram appears upon the dial. However, the internal mechanism of the clock is of a much later period, approximately early eighteenth century.

Romantic Rushen is certainly a castle not to be missed by the visitor and the services of a guide are available to the public in order to explain the history and architecture of this venerable stronghold.

RUSHEN ABBEY AND MONKS BRIDGE

Some two miles north-east of Castletown is the village of Ballasalla with all that remains of the Abbey of St. Mary of Rushen. The name Rushen has been applied to the Castle, the Abbey, the Parish and the sheading in the south of the Island, in which all the others stand. Some believe that it came from St. Russin, a priest who went to Iona. Others believe it to be simply the name of the sheading transferred to the Parish, the Castle and the Abbey.

As with the Castle, the material used for building the Abbey was almost entirely the grey limestone, undressed and with little architectural adornment. The Abbey itself was of cruciform construction but without the usual central tower. However, the north transept had a tower which is still there. Of the nave and the south transept little remains, though there are parts of the old chancel with a fine Norman arch, now bricked up. Some remains of the Priory buildings have survived and one of these houses a museum.

The Abbey stood alongside the lovely stream of Silver Burn and two or three hundred yards upstream from the Abbey, the Crossag, or Monk's Bridge, built in the fourteenth century is still in excellent order. This fine old bridge (the only one anywhere near its age in the whole Island), should certainly be visited.

Of the history of the ruined Abbey little is known save that it was dissolved in the sixteenth century along with all other Priories and Monasteries.

THE MONK'S ROAD

There is little doubt that a very small church preceded the Abbey. In fact one authority claims that the north transept tower shows signs of having been part of such a church. In the late seventeenth century a great deal of the stone was used to build a house for a Deemster Moore. Other houses were then built for the stones from the ruin provided ready-to-hand material. It is said that the Monk's Road from Rushen Abbey to Bishops Court can still be traced. It passed over the packhorse bridge, or Monk's Bridge. Following these traces would make a worthwhile walk for those interested.

THE SILVERDALE GLEN

The Silverdale is a Manx National Glen and open to the public; the lower reaches of the valley are the property of the Manx National Trust. The rock-bedded water of the Silver Burn flows serenely, for the most part, like a ribbon of blue and silver, sparkling between its emerald margins. Where the rock formations create small dams and waterfalls it flows more swiftly, chattering over its stony course down to the sea at Castletown. The Glen is indeed, exceptionally lovely. Apart from the many beautiful, solitary walks through the Glen, among wild flowers in their seasons, there is also a popular amusement park to the north of Ballasalla. Here entertainment is provided by a roundabout driven by a water-wheel, a boating lake, and there is a café, too, with a convenient car park.

THE MARKET SQUARE

In Castletown, apart from the Castle, the most noticeable feature is a Doric column outside the Castle, named the Smelt Monument in memory of one of the most popular Governors of the Island who, after twenty-eight years in office, died at the age of eighty-five. 'The site of this column had formerly been occupied by the ancient Market Crosse and in the year 1617 Margaret Inequane and her son were condemned by the Jury for Life and Death, for the practice of withcraft and burned to death at the Stake close to the Crosse'. Close by is the Dial—a sundial with thirteen faces which is said to tell the hour by the moon as well as by the sun. In addition it tells the

time at various places across the world, in the same way as (but over
a much larger area than), the eight-faced dial on the Promenade at
Douglas. This one was erected in 1720. A similar sundial in the
Museum at Douglas is dated 1774.

THE CHURCH OF ST. MARY

The Church of St. Mary dates from 1826 but is actually a church of
1698 rebuilt. It is not in any way a typical Manx church, having been
built as the adjunct of a garrison. The inside is more interesting, has
several old pews, a number of memorials and a wonderful view
through the plain glass of the southern windows, right out to sea,
across the bay.

CASTLETOWN GRAMMAR SCHOOL

The building which housed in due turn the Academy, King William's
College and finally the Grammar School until the nineteen-thirties,
began life as one of the chapels or small churches, built by the monks
of Rushen Abbey. After the Dissolution of such establishments it
continued for a short time as a place of worship but was later put to
use as a seat of learning. Today it is an ancient monument and thus
officially protected and preserved.

OLD PARLIAMENT HOUSE

Close to the south-east corner of Castle Rushen stands the former
House of Keys, now the Town Hall. It functioned as the Parliament
House until the transference of the Government to Douglas.

A LINK WITH TRAFALGAR

To the right of St. Mary's Church stands a house once occupied by
Captain John William Quilliam of the Royal Navy who served with
Lord Nelson on board the *Victory* at the Battle of Trafalgar. He now
lies buried in the church of the Parish of Arbory.

THE NAUTICAL MUSEUM

Across the harbour, near the footbridge is the Nautical Museum.
The exhibits cover a period from the seventeenth century almost to
the present day thus giving a record which those interested in the sea
will find hard to resist. The chief exhibit is the clipper *Peggy* which
was built in Castletown in 1791. As a survivor of a line of clippers
that were Manx-built and famous in the seventeenth and eighteenth
centuries, the *Peggy* is of the greatest interest and is in exceptionally
good order. It is believed she continued under sail until about 1820.

The story of her discovery and presentation to the Museum is an
unusual one. The ship belonged to Captain George Quayle, and
during her sailing life she was housed in a boat cellar which had an
archway and a small dock leading to the sea; in time the archway

was bricked up and the *Peggy* forgotten so that even the dock was filled in. In 1935 she was rediscovered and at once recognised for what she was—a survival of the typical coastal craft of the sixteenth, seventeenth and eighteenth centuries. Being Manx-built she was presented very promptly to the nation and suitably restored and preserved in her own old home which itself dates from 1789. Since then the Museum has extended its interests to include examples of fishing-vessels and craft of all kinds in the form of models or photographs. Of special interest is the Karran fleet of sea-going ships which were registered at Castletown. There is, additionally, the only known surviving example of a 'nickie's punt', the nickie being a kind of fishing-vessel.

KING WILLIAM'S COLLEGE

Before Britain's 'Sailor King' William IV endowed the College at Castletown with his name—claiming that he had no money to spare to make a more practical and worldly contribution—it was already known as an Academy for education generally and the Clergy in particular.

It developed from a scheme started as long ago as 1663 when Bishop Barrow, arriving to take up his appointment in the Island was appalled by the low level of education even among candidates for Holy Orders. He took possession of two farms, Hango Hill and Ballagilley to form the basis of a trust fund designed to be spent on improving education. The fund increased through the years and although certain grants were offered to Manxmen for education at Universities abroad, few took advantage of this offer. By 1830 the fund had reached £5,000 and this, added to further contributions from the Islanders, launched the College upon a successful career, now distinguished by the name of the Sovereign. Through the 150 years since its foundation the College has grown and from time to time wings have been added and also new departments. Today King William's College is one of the most handsome buildings in the Island, fittingly so, as it is usually the first one noted by visitors.

HANGO HILL

Overlooking the bay and immediately opposite King William's College is Hango Hill on which are the ruins of 'Mount Strange' a late 17th Century Summer House. Here the Manx martyr 'Illiam Dhone' (William Christian) was 'shotte to death' for his part in the Manx Rising of 1651 against the Royalist House of Derby.

One fired in the air, one fired in the hill.
But Illiam McCowle fired straight, fired to kill.
For Illiam McCowle was a man of firm will,
And thy death Illiam Dhone has broken our hearts.

LANGNESS AND FORT ISLAND

Looking east from Castletown one sees Castletown Bay and the Langness Peninsula north of which is Ronaldsway Airport. On the eastern side of the Langness Peninsula and just where it joins the mainland is the little fishing village of Derbyhaven with the bay of Derby Haven between it and the open sea.

The Peninsula is a bird sanctuary and has a golf course. Down by Dreswick Point is a round tower which is said to date from the early nineteenth century. Variously described as a 'look-out tower' and a 'herring-tower', it was possibly the former during the Napoleonic wars and the latter afterwards. As a 'herring look-out' it would have been very useful for it enabled the fishermen to spot approaching herring shoals.

There is a lighthouse at the extreme southern point of Langness which can be made the objective for a most interesting walk. The shores of the Peninsula are of much greater interest than might be supposed, especially on the western side, where the sea has cut into the softer rocks carving a series of fantastic arcades and grottoes and other strange formations. Of interest here is the Scarlett Nature Trail.

At the north-eastern extremity of the Peninsula is St. Michael's or Fort Island, joined to Langness by a causeway built in the eighteenth century. On the island is a small chapel (probably of the twelfth century), which is said to stand upon the site of a Celtic Keill; the chapel is now a ruin. Close by is the circular stone fort built in the sixteenth century and reconditioned during the Civil War. In 1645 it was named Derby Fort. The initials above the door are said to be those of the seventh Earl who reconditioned the Fort during the Civil War.

DERBYHAVEN AND THE EPSOM DERBY

In the late seventeenth century the forerunner of the present Epsom Derby horse-race was run on the stretch of sand which joins the peninsula and the mainland. It was run first in expectation of improving the local breed of horses and continued so until the end of period in which the Derby family were Lords of Man. The first race of all took place, probably, around the year 1630 and there is a set of rules dated 'July 12th, 1669' still to be seen.

The village of Derbyhaven is a very small place but a wonderful one for anyone wanting a quiet holiday. In the twelfth century the Vikings used to drag their boats across the narrow neck of land separating Castletown Bay from Derby Haven because, if the weather was rough, launching was impossible at Castletown. It is said that Ronaldsway gets its name from the Viking Ragnald, or Ronald, who was responsible for organising this particular short cut!

Northwards the picturesque, rocky coast continues to the mouth of the Silver Burn and its Glen. Inland the terrain rises gradually towards the rolling central hills.

CASTLETOWN TO DOUGLAS

THE WALKER, IF HE KEPT religiously to the coast between Castletown and Douglas would have to cover some twelve miles of virtually rockbound seaboard; he would pass the mouths of two very beautiful glens, the Santon and the Grenaugh and would also see much that a motorist must miss. Once he had reached Port Soderick, such a walker would perforce have to rejoin and tramp along the coast road for this is where it follows very closely the edge of the cliffs into Douglas.

THE 'LITTLE PEOPLE'

The direct motor road to Douglas follows very much the same route as the Victorian Railway. If the motorist forks left at Ballaquaggan in order to avoid the coastal route, he will shortly cross the Santon Burn by a bridge. On Ordnance Survey Map number 87, Grid Reference SC 305719 it is shown clearly as 'Fairy Bridge' for it is close to this spot that the 'Little People' of Man have their headquarters. Now, it is a time-honoured custom among Manxmen to pay due respect to these 'other' Manx folk by the raising of hats to wish them a 'very good day' whenever crossing the bridge. This is not a custom 'more honoured in the breach than the observance'! Quite the contrary in fact, for a surprising number of modern Manxmen would not dream of offending the 'Little People' by neglecting this courtesy. These strange little beings, whether they exist or not, have played a considerable part in the Manx heritage.

MALEW PARISH CHURCH

The motorist leaving Castletown by the road going north to Foxdale, comes first to the road junction known as Cross Four Ways, and a short distance before the junction is the Malew Parish Church, named for St. Lua, a Celtic holy man. This church is held to be a very good example of the old Manx type of religious edifice and the nave, which is probably the oldest part of the building is of the twelfth or thirteenth century.

The north transept is a modern addition to allow for the seating of troops from the garrison. It will be noticed that the bellropes hang down outside the door and this is an old Manx custom unlikely to be found elsewhere. There is also a Runic Cross with a scene from the story of Sigurd while the font is possibly older than the Church. Inside there are memorials to a great many members of fairly well-known Manx families. This is one of the few really old, typical Manx churches and should not be missed by anyone with a love for plain simple design in architecture.

TO FOXDALE

Northwards from the Cross Four Ways the road climbs gently through pleasant countryside up to an altitude of 500 ft. to the village of Ballamodha. Here a right turn may be taken for St. Mark's, a road junction on the A26. The Church of St. Mark was erected in 1772 and close by it is the site of the 'Black Fort' of Sir Walter Scott's romance *Peveril of the Peak*.

The main Foxdale road, A4, however, continues directly northward, still climbing gently to pass through the plantations on the slopes of South Barrule and the Stony Mountain before it reaches the pleasant little village of Foxdale.

A left turn at the Cross Four Ways would take the motorist on an alternative run through good farming country and by the villages of Ballabeg, and Colby to Port St. Mary and Port Erin. Northwards from this road and to the east and west of the Foxdale road there are a number of attractive side roads and lanes which will enable the tourist to explore the lesser known countryside of the region. Two particularly pleasant routes are as follows: firstly, north from Ballabeg to Ronague where fork right over the hills to the reservoir in the Cringle Plantation on the south-west slopes of South Barrule, then on to the Foxdale road, the A4; secondly, take a left fork, less than a mile north of the Cross Four Ways and continue uphill to the southern buttress of South Barrule where a further left turn will lead to Ballabeg and a right turn thereafter for the Foxdale road.

Farther east, the Ballasalla–St. Marks' road enables the motorist to see much of the countryside, for the triangle of gently sloping hills between Castletown, Douglas and St. John's is a delightful area which offers variety around every corner and provides first-class views from most of the high points to be found north of St. Mark's and west of Crosby.

CASTLETOWN TO DOUGLAS BY THE COAST ROAD

FROM CASTLETOWN TO DOUGLAS is a very fine run. Make the journey slowly, otherwise many of the best views and scenes will be missed. The route goes from Castletown to Ballasalla, passing near Ronaldsway Airport and not far from Silver Burn. From Ballasalla it is two miles to Ballaquaggan where the road bears right, this time missing the Fairy Bridge, but crossing the Santon Glen almost immediately after the turn.

The Santon Glen, especially in its lower reaches near the coast is particularly rugged and very beautiful. This is one of the many Manx Glens which should not on any account be missed.

PORT SOLDRICK

Just over a mile beyond the crossing of the Santon Burn a narrow
road leads to the south-west and Santon Church which was dedicated
to St. Santan. The name at that time was spelt Sanctan. This church
was referred to as long ago as the eleventh century but by the
eighteenth century it had been completely rebuilt. Not far from the
church door is the Great Stone under which are buried several
members of the Cosnahan family, all clergymen.

After leaving the church the road continues uphill to end at
Arragon Veg where there are some superb views of the coast. Beyond
Arragon Veg a roughish path leads on to a sandy beach between two
rock-girt headlands. This is a quiet and little-used cove which should
prove a gem to those who seek peace and quiet. It is known as Port
Soldrick and is not to be confused with Port Soderick which is a
sizeable village further north.

PORT GRENAUGH

Continuing along the Douglas road a further half a mile brings the
motorist to another right-hand turn; this road runs the length of the
Grenaugh Glen to a delightful little beach, mostly shingle. It has a
number of caves on its north side. This is Port Grenaugh, pronounced
'Grenack' and noted for its day-long sunshine. A pathway up the cliff
on the northern side of the cove will take the visitor to the site of a
Viking house of the eleventh century, enclosed within the earth walls
and the sheer cliffs of a promontory fort. In the next field is a
reconstruction of the Viking house. The site is now known as
Cronk-ny-Merriu. At the head of the beach is a café.

Up to this point the coastline from Castletown will have been
viewed mainly from a distance by the motorist; only the clifftop walker
will have seen it at all closely. This is a really wonderful shoreline
and a great deal less well-known than the last few miles from Port
Soderick to Douglas, where the road hugs the clifftops religiously.

PORT SODERICK

Over the next three miles to the Port Soderick turning, the road is
some distance from the coast. There are, however, three narrow roads
which give the motorist a chance to see this fine rocky coast closely
as it passes round Santon Head, Pistol Castle and the sharp headland
of the Gob Lhiack before Port Soderick is reached. Once again the
walker gains all the advantages and is able to investigate more
closely the many things of intelrest along the way.

Port Soderick itself is a small cove but equipped with all necessary
amenities to welcome the visitor. There are several very fine caves
which are worth investigation, and there is also a first-class clifftop
walk going southwards to Santon Head affording excellent views of
the coast both to the north and to the south. Alternatively there is a

way through the woods to the west of the village and close to the Crogga River, which joins the sea at this rocky inlet. Both make interesting and delightful walks which can be lengthened or curtailed according to taste.

At Port Soderick the Marine Drive commences and continues almost into Douglas. This quite remarkable piece of road-making is one of the nicest drives around Douglas, giving magnificent views along the coast where, in places, sheer cliffs drop some 300 ft. down to the sea. In a number of places this road bridges gorges with fearful drops below and the whole length has been blasted out of the cliffside. Less than two miles from Douglas the archway across the road proclaims the beginning or the end of the Marine Drive. However, the road continues in exactly the same style to Douglas Head from where some of the finest views can be obtained. From there, one further mile takes the visitor into the town centre of Douglas.

South of the Douglas–Peel road there are many side roads that should attract the motorist and the walker. All lead into the hills which increase gradually in height the further west one travels. Although there is nothing of special note in this area it is, nevertheless, a very beautiful place and the countryside and quiet side roads offer pleasant motoring and considerable peace. Woodland abounds and nature has been very generous. Take the side roads to go exploring.

Douglas Bay

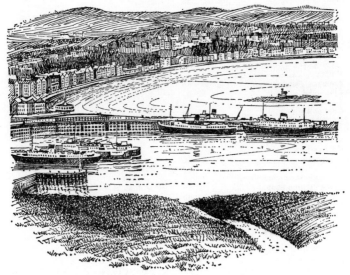

Index

Isle of Man

STREETPLAN

Douglas, Ramsey, Peel,
Port St. Mary, Castletown
and Port Erin

 A Geographia Map

Street plans of the major
towns: Douglas, Ramsey, Peel,
Port St. Mary, Castletown
and Port Erin. Bus routes
and places of interest.

Useful Companions

The ideal map for planning
excursions. Tracks, footpaths
are marked clearly in addition
to the main roads Sandy
beaches, places of interest
also shown.